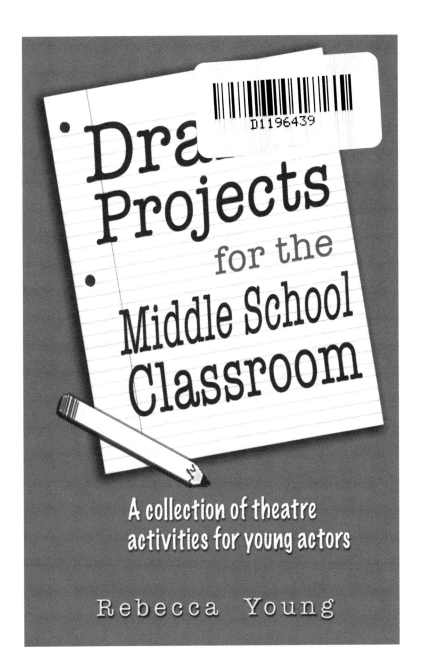

Drama Projects

for the

Middle School

Classroom

A collection of theatre
activities for young actors

Rebecca Young

MERIWETHER PUBLISHING
A division of Pioneer Drama Service, Inc.
Denver, Colorado

Meriwether Publishing
A division of Pioneer Drama Service, Inc.
PO Box 4267
Englewood, CO 80155

www.pioneerdrama.com

Editor: Theodore O. Zapel
Assistant editor: Nicole Rutledge
Cover design: Jan Melvin

Library of Congress Cataloging-in-Publication Data

Young, Rebecca, 1965-
  Drama projects for the middle school classroom : a collection of theatre activities for young actors / by Rebecca Young. -- First edition.
      pages cm
   ISBN 978-1-56608-191-7 (pbk.)
   1. Improvisation (Acting) 2. Acting--Study and teaching (Middle school) 3. Theater--Study and teaching (Middle school) 4. Drama in education. I. Title.
   PN2071.I5Y68 2013
   372.66—dc23

                                        2012047226

3   4   16

This book is dedicated to new beginnings.
Just as this book was my first adventure into drama projects,
you never know where life is going to take you.
Go with the flow and enjoy the ride!

Table of Contents

Introduction

There's so much more to drama class than just teaching students how to act! Working on individual and group projects devoted to drama components helps students learn everything that the world of drama encompasses. From costumes, scenery, and props to commentating, creative writing, and character development, there's a whole array of skills that can be developed and investigated. Maybe after doing a project on props, a student discovers he or she really likes the "behind the scenes" aspect of drama instead of being in the spotlight.

Drama Projects for the Middle School Classroom is a great addition for any drama teacher who wants to provide alternative ways to develop unique drama-related skills. Oh, and did I mention that they can be *fun,* too? Most projects can be modified to be an individual or a group project and can take from one to five class periods, depending on how much time you want to devote to a particular topic or component. Some chapters include worksheets for the students to complete on their own or in a group.

Don't worry, if the original project idea doesn't grab you, each project has a list of ideas to "add on" to the project or a suggestion (or two) on how you can vary the project to suit your needs. In addition, each project section has "Tips and Tricks" to help guide you and/or the student and a "Fun Facts" section just for ... you guessed it ... *fun!*

So what are you waiting for? It's time to start a drama project!

Chapter 1
Mary Poppins and Her Bag of Tricks

Chapter Objective

Help students use ordinary items to develop specific character traits, product advertisements, or scenes. Promotes creativity, character development, scene and dialogue writing skills, and, if group activity is selected, teamwork.

Activity Overview

Fill a sack with odd items that are completely unrelated. (See page 8 for ideas.) Make sure to include both typically gender-specific items and non-gender-specific items. Number of items depends on variation selected below.

Project Timeline

This project can take anywhere between one and five class periods depending on the variation selected. If writing a commercial or scene, allow at least two class periods (possibly three) for brainstorming ideas and writing the script. If acting out, allow another two classes for staging and practice.

Variations of Idea or Add-Ons

✎ Have each student blindly pick three items and then come up with a character based on at least two of those items. Write at least a one-page summary describing the character and how those items fit into his or her life.

Why, you ask? In order for an actor to portray a character well, the character must be three dimensional. In other words, it must have depth. And in order for you, the actor, to become that character, you must *know* that character. It's the details that make a character complete.

Example: I pick three items: a pair of toenail clippers, a wooden spoon, and a washcloth.

A wooden spoon seems obvious. I could easily use it to say that my character gets punished with a wooden spoon every night by her abusive mother or father. Or maybe I could switch it up a little and say it is an aunt or a grandparent. Or, heaven forbid, a mean old teacher. But what fun is that? Creating a character is like creating a life. I hold all the power. Why settle for mundane when I can challenge myself to think beyond the ordinary?

So I settle on the toenail clippers and washcloth. What quirky ways could these two items impact a character? My brain starts ticking. Maybe my character was born with a deformed little toe and because of this has become obsessed with making sure all nine of her other toes look completely perfect at all times. Not a smudge on her polish, a chip from her nail, or an uneven pedicure. All nails trimmed to exactly the same length.

Because of this obsession, my character carries a pair of nail clippers in her pocket as well as a bottle of nail polish and an emery board. My character summary would include details of how embarrassed, ashamed, and self-conscious this has made her feel her entire life. Those clippers have gone from ordinary to extraordinary. They have just become a lifeline to this character, an important detail that shapes my character into someone unique and interesting.

But what about the washcloth? How can I add another ordinary object into my character's life without it seeming too contrived? Well, first of all, remember that life is almost *always* stranger than fiction. Sometimes, when we hear someone's life story, we can't help but think, "That *can't* be true!" But life has a way of being bizarre. Embrace it! Don't be afraid to go all out when you're making your items relate to your character.

What if she keeps a worn-out, ratty old washcloth under her pillow because it's the only thing she has left of her mother's? A mother that just up and left her at only four years old? I can even tie the first issue to this piece of the story by saying that she just knew her mother left her because she wasn't perfect. Her mother was a former beauty queen. Perfection meant everything to her. That's why she didn't stick around. Why would she? "She was ashamed of me. Beauty queens don't have daughters like me."

Get the picture? Even ordinary items can help shape a person's character and tell a story about someone that delves deeper and provides more insight than just giving the standard description of someone. How much more do you know about my character than if I had just told you she was a girl who had a deformed toe and whose mother had left her when she was little? Thinking about the toenail clippers and the washcloth give her depth and meaning. As an actor, would you be able to better portray this character now that you know more about her? Absolutely!

So, when you grab your items out of the bag, squash that voice in your head that immediately goes for the obvious. Think deeper. Imagine and create a character that jumps off the page and comes to life. Provide lots and lots of details. Emotions. Thoughts. History.

Why is your character the way he or she is? When you are finished with your one-page summary (or more if you truly delve deep!), do you know *who* your character is? Would an actor be able to adequately portray the many emotions of your character? Is your character just a series of words on a page, or has he/she actually come to life before your eyes?

✎ Groups of five or more: Have each group pick one item and then develop either a radio advertisement or a television commercial script based on the item. The twist? The item can't be used for its ordinary purpose. For example, a bottle of water can't be for drinking. Brainstorm the possibilities. How can you commercialize that item into a product that could be sold to the masses? But don't take it too seriously. You're using the item for a completely different and unusual purpose — so make it fun!

Example 1: A plastic swim cap.

This item could be sold as a collapsible bowl (a "collapse-a-bowl!") for those moments when you just wish you had your own bowl at hand. A few scenes could make up the commercial where the voiceover person always says something like, "It's times like these when you'll be glad you had your very own stylish and completely portable collapse-a-bowl." And the actor pulls out the bowl from her purse, briefcase, backpack, back pocket, etc.

Scenes could be a restaurant where you see a cockroach crawling across the table, or a parent trying to use those pesky little cardboard boxes of cereal as the bowl and cereal flies everywhere when it's ripped open and destroyed, or maybe it's a kid sneaking a snack during class and the chip bag is too loud and noisy but the collapse-a-bowl is perfect! Think of your commercial as more of a spoof than an actual product presentation and allow your funny side to shine through.

Example 2: A phone book.

Could a phone book's purpose be to help short people reach the water fountain or help the shortest guy in class get a date? Maybe it's the perfect portable stepstool for those people who suffer from "ladder anxiety." (Yeah, I just made that up. But why not? It could happen! Advertisers often make us afraid of things to sell their products. Like getting old or having frizzy hair!)

Think of the phone book as "platform shoes" and go all out! (If you don't know what platform shoes are, ask your parents.)

Follow-up activity: Act out the script or record/perform the radio ad.

✎ Groups of five or more: Have each group select one item and then develop a one- to two-minute family or friend scene (i.e. dialogue script) using that item.

Example 1: Item is a tube of pink lip gloss (or for guys it could be a razor).

Create a family scene where the father is upset that his baby girl (or son — who is in middle school, of course) is looking more and more like a teenager! He thinks lip gloss (or shaving) leads to more makeup, piercings, tattoos, dating, marriage, his daughter moving to another country (or his son joining the military), etc. Make the dad go completely nuts with his exaggerations! Mom takes the opposite approach of how "it's just lip gloss, practically ChapStick," and "it's nothing to burst a blood vessel over." This character is calm as a cucumber, and no amount of hysteria from her husband is going to ruffle her feathers. Siblings, best friends, dear old auntie, etc. could be added in minor roles as needed to accommodate the group size.

Example 2: A partial phone number on a piece of paper.

Create a friend scene where each girl or guy is accusing the other of stealing their girlfriend/boyfriend. Lots of accusations and anger! From where did the number come? Out of whose purse or backpack did it drop? Have different alibis as to what the number is really for — the person's orthodontist, hairdresser, tutor, etc. "I can't help it if the number is *almost* the same as so and so's." Expand on the paranoia of the accuser. Remember: the more dramatic the script, the more fun it will be to act it out!

Follow-up activity: Act out the script, using only the item as a prop.

✎ Have students answer the "Famous Props" activity on page 10.

Tips & Tricks

- Think outside the box: Could your character be an alien, talking animal, or superhero? No one said it has to be human. How would an ordinary item from today impact those types of characters? What about a futuristic character? Or maybe one from the past? How would a character like that misunderstand the purpose of the item?
- For the individual character development assignment, interview your character to provide more depth. (See the Chapter 11 "Character Interview" questions on page 60 for sample questions.) What would he or she tell you about the items you hold in your hand? Ask questions that probe into the psyche of your character. You may be surprised at what you find out.
- When writing your script for your commercial, it may help to watch a few "infomercials" on television. Notice how they keep adding on to the many uses the product has and how you're getting such a great deal when you pay the low, low price of only "$9.99" and you get *"all this!"* Does your product need a gimmick, mascot, or celebrity endorsement? Your options are wide open! Got a famous movie star you want to be your project model? Go for it! Been dying to do a celebrity impersonation? Now's your chance!

Fun Facts

- According to msnbc.msn.com, the infomercial industry is booming, enjoying $91 billion dollars a year in sales, offering safe, reliable products, and making household names out of super pitchmen who offer you products to buy from the comfort of your own home.
- Julie Andrews won the Academy Award for Best Actress for her performance as Mary Poppins, and the film also won Oscars for Best Film Editing, Original Music Score, Best Song for "Chim Chim Cher-ee," and Best Visual Effects, receiving a total of thirteen nominations.
- According to cbcawards.com, author D. Robert Pease says this about his award-winning Young Adult novel, *Noah Zarc:* "Noah being a paraplegic was also not intentional. He actually didn't start

out that way, but I had one of those strange instances where my character 'spoke' to me and said he was a paraplegic. I actually fought it for a while because I didn't want people to think I wrote him that way for some *politically correct* reason. In the end, I gave in because I realized I had no choice; Noah *was* a paraplegic, so I couldn't fight it any more."

Item Ideas

Select items from this list or come up with your own.
Loofah
Barrette, hair clip, bobby pin
Pencil
Calculator
Newspaper
Paperclip
Washcloth
Toothbrush
Cotton ball
Screwdriver
Plastic spoon
Straw
Lotion
Keychain
Flashlight
Men's deodorant
Baby powder
Travel-size shampoo, mouthwash, hairspray, etc.
Sock
Ribbon
Journal
Children's book
Comb or brush
Safety pin
Coupon
Dental floss
Pack of gum
Rubber ball or marble
Any coin
Rock
Nail polish or lipstick
Stamp

Small stuffed animal
Baby bottle or rattle
Cup
Photo
Package of crackers
Receipt
Music CD
Earphones
Piece of gaudy jewelry
Scrap of material
Toenail clippers
Glove or mitten
Umbrella
Grocery bag
Gift bag
Small piece of wrapping paper
Movie ticket stub
Empty picture frame
Plastic army man
Toy car
Deck of cards
Water bottle
Sunscreen
Lollipop
Empty soda can
Spool of thread
Figurine of anything
China plate, cup, bowl, etc.
Fake flower
Ripped out page from a magazine

Famous Props

Sometimes we know a character right away based on a simple prop they carry. Can you name the famous characters below?

1. This character either has or always wants a pot of honey.
2. This *Peanuts* character always carries a blanket.
3. This character wouldn't be anything without his lamp.
4. This famous singer kept only one hand warm with a single white glove.
5. If you're going to portray this character, you'd better buy a patch of fur to make a really hairy chest.
6. This girl couldn't get home if she didn't click her ruby red shoes together.
7. This action hero wouldn't be the same without his whip.
8. This famous alien liked a candy movie prop: Reese's Pieces.
9. This space hero couldn't fight Darth Vader without his light saber.
10. This Greek god can do some serious damage with his oversized hammer.

Famous Props Answers

1. Winnie the Pooh
2. Linus
3. Genie
4. Michael Jackson
5. Austin Powers
6. Dorothy Gale
7. Indiana Jones
8. E.T.
9. Luke Skywalker
10. Thor

Chapter 2
And This Is ...

Chapter Objective

Break the ice! One objective is to get students talking to each other and discovering their similarities and/or differences. Depending on which variation you choose, students are either practicing their acting skills, their creative-writing skills, or both! This is also a great beginning public speaking exercise for those students who aren't ready to jump on-stage. A one-minute introduction of a peer using notes as a guide is less threatening than memorizing lines and staging. If doing the "two truths and a lie" variation, students will be able to practice controlling their facial expressions so that the class cannot tell when they are lying.

Activity Overview

Pair students up and have them interview each other about interesting facts in their life. Not your ordinary, "What's your favorite color?" but interesting tidbits like "What's the strangest pet you've either owned or wished you had?" (See pages 16-17 for sample questions.) Then, take turns standing up and introducing the other person to the class. *Key objective:* Find out interesting and quirky things that will make the person's introduction stand out and get the audience's attention. They might want to start with, "Something you may not know about ..." This is a good icebreaker activity to do at the first of the year or semester when students don't know much about each other.

Project Timeline

This project will take one to two class periods depending on the size of the class. Allow at least ten minutes for each interview (twenty minutes for the pair). Each introduction will take about a minute.

Variations of Idea or Add-Ons

✎ Have the students perform the interview instead of the introduction. Take turns so that each person has the opportunity to be the commentator who performs the professional interview.

✎ Let the introduction be for a "future you." If the interview was held twenty years in the future, what responses would the students give? In other words, what would be their fantasy life? What kind of career would they have? Family? Riches? Fame? Or would they be living in a remote jungle finding a cure for cancer from a newly-discovered plant species? (See page 17 for sample questions.)

✎ Want to show them how a pro does it? Show an old Barbara Walters interview in class. Have students take notes on the types of questions that a professional interviewer asks. What would they have done differently? Were there questions that were missed or avoided? What questions were boring or obvious?

✎ Pair students up where one is the interviewer and the other is a famous celebrity. Use one or two class periods for research where the pair works together to find real facts about the celebrity to be used in the performance. For fun, allow students to add in a few untruths and see if the class can figure out which facts are true and which ones are false!

✎ Two truths and a lie: Instead of an interview scenario, have students introduce their partner with "two truths and a lie." After they've interviewed the person about some wild and wacky things in their life, they select two real items and create a third item that is completely untrue. For example, "John has played the electric piano since he was five years old." This may or may not be true. The idea is for the lie to be somewhat believable so that it isn't clearly the untruth. The class then guesses which one of the three "facts" is the lie.

As an acting review, have the class provide feedback on how the "lie" was presented. Did the speaker's face give it away, or was he or she able to control the emotions and keep a "poker face" while delivering all three statements? In poker, it's called a "tell" when a person's face or body movements give them away. (A "tell" is any clue, habit, behavior, or physical reaction that gives other players more information about your hand.) What "tells" did the speaker have, if any?

Teach students not to provide "tells" when saying the statement that is untrue or to use a "tell" to their advantage. Often a "tell" is used to throw someone off the scent. For example, on one of the truth statements, I may act more nervous or shift my eyes around to make you think that I'm lying, when I'm really telling the truth. According to playwinningpoker.com, there are ten major "tells." Only seven really apply to what we're talking about, so let's look at them:

1. **Watch the eyes** — It takes practice to look someone in the eye while being "dishonest." In this case, actors need to remember they are "playing a part" — not lying. This will make it easier to face the audience head-on and not those shifty eyes.
2. **Facial expression** — Try not to let your face change during the "lie." Keep your expression even. Definitely don't look downward like you can't face the audience.
3. **Weak is strong and strong is weak** — Don't overdo the acting. For instance, being overly nonchalant on the statement that is untrue is just as telling as being overly confident.
4. **Anxiety** — Don't let your anxiousness show. Some people's voices will rise or they will experience a dry throat.
5. **Trembling hands** — If you can't help shaking from nerves, make sure you shake on all the statements and not just the lie. Unfortunately for new actors, this isn't usually a problem!
6. **Glance at "chips"** — Or in this case, your notes. Make sure you don't give away the lie by having to read the statement word for word.

7. Body posture/attitude — Don't show an obvious change in body posture/stance when presenting the statements, unless you do it on purpose to trick the audience. For instance, slumping more during the lie may make the audience think that you're uncomfortable telling a lie.

✎ "Was that a question?" This is best done using the class as a whole. Have everyone stand in a circle facing each other. Then have one person start a conversation with the person next to them by asking a question. The person then has to respond in question form as well, either to the first person or to the person to the other side of them. Questions can be unrelated, but when they become related is when the fun really starts. The way that you get out is if you respond with anything but a question, if you respond with a one-word answer or question like "what?" or if you repeat a question from either yourself or another person.

To make it fun, it needs to move fast!
Example: Person 1 — "What is your name?" Person 2 — "When do we get out of school?" Person 3 — "What time is it?" And so on until someone messes up and answers the question or does something else that would get them "out."

✎ Acronym antics: Young actors are often afraid to even open their mouths in a classroom, much less act. Use this icebreaker activity to open up those hesitant students. Description: Create a list of four-letter words. (Definitely don't ask the students to create a list of four-letter words or you could be in trouble!) These can be any words at all. Here are a few to get you started: ring, left, hand, play, tune, head, call, clip, coin. This game is played by assuming each word is an acronym. Players must create definitions for the acronym on the fly by saying the first word out of their mouths. So, for example, the definition for "ring" might end up as "Randy is nice guy," with each word in the sentence being contributed by a different player. There is, however, a pattern to the definition. The first word is typically a noun or a name of someone, the second word is usually a verb, the third word is usually an adjective, and the fourth word is typically another noun. To start the game, point to a player and say the word. For example: "left." The player then starts by saying the first noun they can think of starting with "L" such as lizards. The person on their left then must say the first verb they can think of starting with "E" such as "eat." The next person says an adjective starting with "F" such as "flowery" and finally the last person finishes with "tarts" which starts with "T." So the final sentence is "Lizards eat flowery tarts." The sillier the better! The key to the game is to get players to say the first words that come to mind and to move the game along quickly. After one sentence is done, move quickly to the next player and throw out another word. This is great for laughs! If players mess up and don't say anything for about five seconds, they are out.

✎ Have students complete the "I Talked to Barbara Walters" word scramble on page 18.

Tips & Tricks

- You can provide questions for the students to use in interviewing if you want to offer more structure. (See pages 16-17.)
- Is the person you're interviewing the most boring person in the world? Is listening to their life story worse than watching paint dry? How can you as an actor spice up the presentation to make even the most boring responses come to life? Can you take on an accent? Be melodramatic? Add humor or tragedy to the most mundane details? Or can you be so droll delivering the introduction that the delivery is funny and entertaining?
- Spend time practicing using "tells" to your advantage. Can you confuse the audience by making them think you're lying when you're not? What can be your "tell" that you *want* the audience to notice? (i.e., biting your lip, shifting your feet, talking a little louder during the "lie" statement, etc.)

Fun Facts

- According to biography.com, Barbara Walters won her first Daytime Entertainment Emmy Award for best host in a talk series in 1975.
- In Colorado in 2009, Richard Heene created a fake news story involving his six-year-old son and an out-of-control, homemade flying weather balloon. He allowed the public and news media to believe his son was trapped in the runaway balloon to gain fame and get his family onto a reality show. When it was discovered that the boy was hiding and the entire story was fake, Heene faced criminal charges. (Watch the coverage on YouTube and see if you can tell that he's lying.)
- According to design-laorosa.com, the *Star Trek* TV programs and films have inspired many of today's technological achievements. The design of real-life flip (or "clamshell") phones is directly based on that of Starfleet communicators.
- Oprah Winfrey is said to be one of the best interviewers of all times. In 2007, Forbes magazine estimated her pay at $260 million. Her estimated worth was $1.5 billion.

Interview Questions (Normal Version)

1. Who is your favorite cartoon character? Why?
2. If you were a vampire and couldn't go out at night, what would your hobbies be?
3. What is the weirdest food you've ever tasted?
4. What's the worst thing you've ever done?
5. Who would you say is your "celebrity twin"? Who is the famous person that you most closely resemble? (You have to pick someone!)
6. If you had to pick a piece of clothing that represents who you are, what would it be and why?
7. Who is your favorite person? If you were to wake up as that person tomorrow, what is the first thing you would do?
8. If you were to get a henna tattoo today, what would it be and why?
9. Tell me something that you absolutely hate doing. Why?
10. What is one thing that drives you crazy?
11. Would you rather live underwater like a mermaid (or merman) or would you rather live on another planet? Why?
12. Would you rather have a real Transformers car or have your own personal airplane? Why?

13. If you were your own parent, what is one rule you would get rid of? What is one rule you would impose?
14. What is one thing you have in your room/house that you don't think anyone else has?
15. What is the one thing that makes you different from everyone else?

Interview Questions (Futuristic Version)

Imagine how your life will be twenty years from now. You are the author of your life so you can be and do anything you want. With that in mind, answer the following:

1. Tell me about a typical day at your job.
2. Do you have children? How many?
3. A fireplace mantle is a great place to show off trophies and awards. Imagine your mantle. What awards do you have on display?
4. Many people thought that in the year 2000 people would be living in futuristic Jetson-style homes. What does your home look like? What does your car look like?
5. Everyone makes mistakes. What do you think yours would be? What is the one thing you would do differently? What advice would you give yourself at the age you are now?
6. Tell me about your financial status. How did you make your money and what do you do with it?
7. Do you have pets? What kind and how many? What are their names?
8. Are you married? Describe the dream wedding that you had.
9. Where is the most exciting place that you have traveled? What did you do there?
10. Kids love toys. So do adults. What grown-up toys do you own? (i.e., boat, motorcycle, RV, electronics, etc.)

I Talked to Barbara Walters

In her career, Barbara Walters interviewed many famous people, including actors, singers, politicians, world leaders, and more. Can you unscramble the names of some of the people below who underwent this famous interviewer's scrutiny?

1. mosin llewco _____

2. eevst objs _____

3. ramgrate tatcherh _____

4. ifeld acsrot _____

5. saahr alpin _____

6. cimhela ajcsonk _____

7. ibll agtes _____

8. ddaonl pturm _____

9. asdnar kublloc _____

10. tetby hweit _____

11. gtier owosd _____

12. liwl shmit _____

13. mot rcusie _____

14. tleon hjon _____

15. amkr uzkecrbreg _____

I Talked to Barbara Walters Hints
Want to make it easier for your students to figure these out? Provide these hints if desired!

1. Television judge
2. Creator of Apple
3. Longest-serving Prime Minister of the United Kingdom
4. Cuban communist revolutionary and politician
5. Politician, author, and speaker (extra hint: Actress Tina Fey looks just like her!)
6. Singer
7. Founder of Microsoft
8. Business magnate
9. Actress
10. Actress
11. Golf pro
12. Actor
13. Actor
14. Singer
15. Creator of Facebook

I Talked to Barbara Walters Answers
1. Simon Cowell
2. Steve Jobs
3. Margaret Thatcher
4. Fidel Castro
5. Sarah Palin
6. Michael Jackson
7. Bill Gates
8. Donald Trump
9. Sandra Bullock
10. Betty White
11. Tiger Woods
12. Will Smith
13. Tom Cruise
14. Elton John
15. Mark Zuckerberg

Chapter 3
Magazine Mania

Chapter Objective

Students will use creative thinking to turn a "still" or a photograph into a story. Writing skills and acting skills are utilized in this activity.

Activity Overview

Pick any magazine and find an ad that has at least one person or animal. Write the dialogue for a one-minute scene based on what you see and what you don't see, even if it means you've got talking cats or dogs! Include characters not depicted in the advertisement. Who else would come on scene based on the episode unfolding? Is your scene a comedy, tragedy, dramatic moment, or just a day in an ordinary life?

Note: Don't have a supply of magazines on hand? Have the students bring some in or have them find their own ad at home. If that doesn't work, pull up online ads in your classroom and have them pick one. Or if you're really brave, just bring in some old family snapshots. The students will definitely have fun writing your family history!

Project Timeline

This project can take anywhere between one and five class periods, depending on the variation selected. If writing a commercial or scene, allow at least two class periods (possibly three) for brainstorming ideas and writing the script. If acting out, allow another two classes for staging and practice.

Variations of Idea or Add-Ons

✎ Do as an individual or group project when writing the dialogue. If adding on the acting piece, do in groups of at least three or four.

✎ Write a prop list for everything you see in the ad. Also include a detailed description of where the ad was filmed (i.e., the scenery).

✎ Instead of a scene with multiple characters, what if you only hear the viewpoint of one character? Write a monologue for the main character in the advertisement. The purpose isn't to sell the product, but to bring the character to life using the product/scene shown in the advertisement.

✎ As a class, brainstorm every movie or television show that used (or uses) an obviously sponsored product. (For example, the television reality show *American Idol* clearly displays Coca Cola products on the judges' table.)

✎ Instead of writing a new scene, write a radio ad that would complement the print advertisement. This time, it's all about the selling! How can you convert a print ad into an audio version where the listeners can't see the product? How will you describe it so that listeners want to buy it?

✎ Design a secondary ad. Can you make a completely different ad by changing the timeframe (i.e., past or future), setting (i.e., different planet, fantasy world, desert instead of ocean, etc.), or characters?

✎ Or maybe the ad you've found sets the stage for a series of ads that tells a story. Not sure what I mean? Research the Taster's Choice coffee ads from the past that created a short melodrama in a series of advertisements. It was like watching a mini soap opera. In the 1990s, Taster's Choice coffee began running serialized commercial spots starring British actors Sharon Maughan and Anthony Head that followed the romantic encounters of a man and a woman who shared a fondness for Taster's Choice. The commercials created a soap opera environment which enticed and teased the viewers to tune in to the next commercial to see whether the attractive couple would progress beyond just sharing a cup of coffee to possibly sharing a date. The successful commercial spots produced a ten percent increase in product sales soon after they aired, according to TVacres.com.

Tips & Tricks

- Don't settle on the first ad you see. Flip through several magazines before you pick the final one.
- Not sure how to turn a product advertisement into a scene? Think about any show or movie you watch — every scene uses products! In fact, product placements, or embedded advertising, are a huge part of movies and television shows. It's called subliminal advertising when they place items and don't specifically draw your attention to them. Some placements are meant to be subliminal, though. Check out the list in the "Fun Facts" section to see how often product placements are used in prime time shows. How do those products play into the scene? Watch an episode of your favorite show and write down any object picked up or used in the scene. How could you manipulate a scene to be about that object?
- Scene writing tip: Make things difficult for your character! It adds tension. Then keep upping the ante. The second obstacle is worse than the first, etc. Then, resolution.
- Remember: Characters want things. And characters have problems. Two key elements in writing a scene.
- Don't just pick any name for your character. Really think about a name that fits your character's personality.

Fun Facts

- Audi had a futuristic-looking model made for the movie *I, Robot* (2004) as a product placement for their brand.
- In the *Back to the Future* trilogy, Pizza Hut's products in 2015 include an instant pizza that can be hydrated for immediate consumption. Pepsi is also seen throughout the movies.
- In the game *Need for Speed: Most Wanted*, there are several images of Burger King, such as billboards and restaurants.
- According to CNBC.com, here are the top ten prime time shows with the most product placements in 2011:

10. *The Amazing Race* — Product placement occurrences: 161, Episodes in 2011: 11, Network: CBS
 9. *America's Next Top Model* — Product placement occurrences: 178, Episodes in 2011: 26, Network: CW
 8. *Friday Night Lights* — Product placement occurrences: 201, Episodes in 2011: 13, Network: NBC
 7. *America's Got Talent* — Product placement occurrences: 220, Episodes in 2011: 32, Network: NBC
 6. *Extreme Makeover: Home Edition* — Product placement occurrences: 224, Episodes in 2011: 31, Network: ABC
 5. *The X Factor* — Product placement occurrences: 312, Episodes in 2011: 26, Network: FOX
 4. *Dancing with the Stars* — Product placement occurrences: 390, Episodes in 2011: 29, Network: ABC
 3. *Celebrity Apprentice* — Product placement occurrences: 391, Episodes in 2011: 12, Network: NBC
 2. *The Biggest Loser* — Product placement occurrences: 533, Episodes in 2011: 34, Network: NBC
 1. *American Idol* — Product placement occurrences: 577, Episodes in 2011: 39, Network: FOX

(For fun, can you think of a product that is featured in the shows listed? Watch one episode and count how many times you see the product appear on camera!)

Chapter 4
Where Can I Find ... ?

Chapter Objective

For those more interested in the backstage arena, this chapter focuses on the props and scenery. By using research skills, students will create prop lists, including a budget for all items necessary in a scene. Students will also learn to think critically in terms of substituting cheaper alternatives when their production is on a budget. This is also a good time to teach students about anachronisms in literature and movies.

Activity Overview

Read a scene from your favorite book and create a prop list. *(Variation: Teacher reads the same scene for the whole class.)* From where would you obtain the items? Which ones would you need to make/create? Think critically: If the scene takes place in a kitchen, what props are generally found there? Picture the scene in your mind and fill in the gaps. When watching a movie, think of all the little items that make a scene believable! Unless it is part of the plot, you don't typically find your characters in a bare or empty room.

Project Timeline

This project can take between one and two class periods depending on if you practice with a television show or movie first (which is recommended). Time allotted also depends on availability of research materials (i.e., computers with Internet, shopping catalogs, etc.). You may have to take the class to the library or computer lab for research.

Variations of Idea or Add-Ons

✎ To prepare for the project, have students watch a few minutes of a television show or movie. Stop and have them write down everything they remember from the scene. Replay the scene and let them add more items to their list. Replay it again. Are they still missing items? Think about a two-hour-long movie and how long the prop list and scenery list would be!

✎ Using the Internet, "shop" online and create a photo book or scrapbook of the items you'll need. Make sure to note the prices of each item.

✎ Provide students with a specific budget and keep it relatively small so that they have to think creatively. They are to track all costs and prepare a prop list. It would be so easy to just purchase everything, but even large productions have a budget. Will students need to make some items in order to stay within their budget? If so, make sure all costs are included. (Glue, thread, material, paint, markers, etc.)

✎ If using the same scene for the whole class, do a review after all groups have presented. What items were overlooked? Were there any stand-out items that a group presented that really made the scene? Were there any props not specifically mentioned or alluded to that could've been present? Again, it's the little things that make a scene more believable.

✎ Has your state been used in a famous movie or television show? Have students do the research to find out!

✎ Teach students about anachronisms: something or someone that is not in its correct historical or chronological time, especially a thing or person that belongs to an earlier time. For example, a movie has a caveman, and the caveman is wearing a watch. Play a film that contains blatant anachronisms, like Disney's *The Emperor's New Groove* or *Hercules,* and either point out the anachronisms or have the students find them. (Hint: The Disney movie *Aladdin* in particular featured many short scenes in which the Genie briefly changed into caricatures of many famous people from all across time, including many 20th-century figures and comedians, and he quoted lines for comic effect. Also, Disney's movie *Hercules* shows ancient Greece with modern-day things and places such as restaurants. Hermes is shown wearing sunglasses and playing on a piano (which does not exist until Italy in the early 1700s). The same goes for Disney's *The Emperor's New Groove,* but this time in the Incan Empire with modern-day things such as restaurants, piñatas, floor washers, scientists' labs, rangers, scouts, teddy bears, roller coasters, levers, candles, toasts, and others. What a fun class project! Watch one of the abovementioned movies and make a list of all the anachronisms!

Tips & Tricks

- Spend some time watching your favorite shows as if you were the prop manager. When you really concentrate on the props and not the dialogue or action, are you amazed at how many little things make up a scene? Prop managers know that it's all about the details!
- Not sure what a scene needs? Walk around your own house. What do you see in common rooms like the kitchen, living room, or bathroom?
- Sales ads are a great place to find items for your prop scrapbook.

Fun Facts

- The fifteen most profitable movies of all time according to CNBC.com:
  15. *The Lord of the Rings: The Return of the King* (2003): Return on investment: 1,008%, Budget: $111 million (inflation-adjusted), Gross revenue: $1.1 billion
  14. *Mrs. Doubtfire* (1993): Return on investment: 1,160%, Budget: $38 million (inflation-adjusted), Gross revenue: $441 million
  13. *There's Something About Mary* (1998): Return on investment: 1,194%, Budget: $31 million (inflation-adjusted), Gross revenue: $370 million
  12. *The Hangover* (2009): Return on investment: 1,297%, Budget: $36 million (inflation-adjusted), Gross revenue: $467 million
  11. *Jaws* (1975): Return on investment: 1,308%, Budget: $36 million (inflation-adjusted), Gross revenue: $471 million
  10. *Ghost* (1990): Return on investment: 1,446%, Budget: $35 million (inflation-adjusted), Gross revenue: $506 million
  9. *Home Alone* (1990): Return on investment: 1,590%, Budget: $30 million (inflation-adjusted), Gross revenue: $477 million
  8. *The Passion of the Christ* (2004): Return on investment: 1,749%, Budget: $35 million (inflation-adjusted), Gross revenue: $612 million

7. *American Beauty* (1999): Return on investment: 1,780%, Budget: $20 million (inflation-adjusted), Gross revenue: $356 million
6. *Star Wars* (1977): Return on investment: 1,938%, Budget: $40 million (inflation-adjusted), Gross revenue: $775 million
5. *Grease* (1978): Return on investment: 1,975%, Budget: $20 million (inflation-adjusted), Gross revenue: $394 million
4. *Pretty Woman* (1990): Return on investment: 2,013%, Budget: $23 million (inflation-adjusted), Gross revenue: $463 million
3. *Slumdog Millionaire* (2008): Return on investment: 2,520%, Budget: $15 million (inflation-adjusted), Gross revenue: $378 million
2. *E.T. the Extra-Terrestrial* (1982): Return on investment: 3,172%, Budget: $25 million (inflation-adjusted), Gross revenue: $793 million
1. *My Big Fat Greek Wedding* (2002): Return on investment: 6,150%, Budget: $6 million (inflation-adjusted), Gross revenue: $369 million

- The film *Grounding,* which is about the collapse of an aircraft, is set in September of the year 2001, yet shows the use of Windows XP, which was not yet released.
- In the movie *Titanic,* Jack (played by Leonardo DiCaprio) mentions that he has gone ice-fishing on Lake Wissota near Chippewa Falls, Wisconsin. However, Lake Wissota is a man-made reservoir which was not created until five years after the Titanic tragedy.
- In *Pirates of the Caribbean: The Curse of the Black Pearl,* Captain Jack Sparrow (played by Johnny Depp) can be seen wearing an Adidas cap in a few scenes.
- The 1995 hit film *Apollo 13* contains numerous errors, including a wrong NASA logo and the appearance of The Beatles' *Let It Be* album a month before it was released.
- Comedy fiction set in the past may use anachronism for humorous effect. One of the first major films to use anachronism was Buster Keaton's *Three Ages,* which included the invention of Stone Age baseball and modern traffic problems in classical Rome.
- Scenery can make or break a movie. Do you know where these famous movies were filmed?
  Raiders of the Lost Ark and *Star Wars* — Tunisia
  Lord of the Rings — New Zealand
  Mama Mia — Greece
  The Man with the Golden Gun — Thailand
  Jurassic Park — Hawaii
  The Grudge — Japan
  The Twilight Saga: New Moon — Italy

Chapter 5
What Did They Say?

Chapter Objective

Students will practice scene writing and dubbing skills to create a "Gag Dub," which promotes humorous interpretation.

According to Wikipedia.org, dubbing is the post-production process of recording and replacing voices on a motion picture or television soundtrack subsequent to the original shooting. The term most commonly refers to the substitution of the voices of the actors shown on the screen by those of different performers, who may be speaking a different language.

The procedure was sometimes practiced in musicals when the actor had an unsatisfactory singing voice and remains in use to enable the screening of audio-visual material to a mass audience in countries where viewers do not speak the same language as the original performers.

"Dubbing" also describes the process of an actor re-recording lines spoken during filming in order to improve audio quality or reflect dialogue changes. This process is called "Automated Dialogue Replacement," "Additional Dialogue Recording," or "ADR" for short. Music is also dubbed onto a film after editing is completed. Dubbing has also been used for comedic purposes, replacing lines of dialogue to create comedies from footage that was originally another genre.

Redubbing is the practice of removing all of the dialogue from an existing movie or television show, and replacing it with an entirely new recording, usually for comedic purposes. Sometimes, rather than attempt to recreate the original dialogue, the copyright holders will simply replace the entire thing with new dialogue to humorous effect — a "Gag Dub."

Activity Overview

Dubbing/Voiceover project: Have students find a clip from their favorite show. (YouTube is a great place to find clips.) Mute the sound and come up with new dialogue for the scene. Students can choose to do a scene or commercial.

Project Timeline

This project can take anywhere between one and five class periods depending on the variation selected. If writing a commercial or scene, allow at least two class periods (possibly three) for brainstorming ideas and writing the script. If acting out, allow another two classes for staging and practice.

Variations of Idea or Add-Ons

✎ Ask the students to do the project individually so they have to depict the different voices *or* let them do it in groups so that each student plays a part.

✎ Write the dialogue for a Sunday comic strip instead, but expand the length to create a whole scene and not just a few frames. They don't have to draw the frames; they just need to write the scene.

✎ Have students create a "top ten" list of their favorite actors who do voiceovers for animated characters. As a follow-up, have them create a website or poster to present to the class. (Just don't let them use the same ones from the "I Know That Voice!" activity.)

✎ Students may complete the "I Know That Voice!" activity on page 30.

Tips & Tricks

- Want to see redubbing in action to give your students an idea of how it's done? Share an old Godzilla film or old martial arts film with the class.
- The easiest way to teach students how to redub a scene is to have students create subtitles for the scene that do not match the original dialogue. If you want, you can stop there and not have students act them out.
- Want to see a professional do it? Watch an old episode of *Whose Line Is It Anyway?* (A popular improv show hosted by Drew Carey. YouTube should have plenty of clips from which to choose.)

Fun Facts

- The initial American release of the movie *Mad Max* had all of the dialogue redubbed by American actors, without the Australian accents.
- There are more Godzilla movies (28) than James Bond movies (22)!
- Lauren Bacall was the voiceover for Fancy Feast cat food in the 90s.
- David Duchovny from the *X-Files* was the voice of a dog in a Pedigree dog food advertisement. One of the catchphrases was, "Rub my belly. Seriously. Rub it."
- Another dog voiceover was done by Zach Braff from *Scrubs* when he provided the voice of a dog in a Cottonelle toilet paper commercial.
- Did you know it was Patrick Dempsey's voice from *Grey's Anatomy* on some of the Mazda "Zoom Zoom" ads?
- Morgan Freeman has been the voice of many Visa commercials.
- Feeling like pizza? Maybe it's because of Queen Latifah's voiceover work in Pizza Hut commercials.

I Know That Voice!

Don't you hate it when you see an animated character with a voice you recognize and yet you can't put a name to the voice? See how well you do at remembering who played these famous characters!

Who played ...
1. Lumiere in *Beauty and the Beast?*
2. Darling, Peg, Si, and Am in *Lady and the Tramp?*
3. Bernard in *The Rescuers?*
4. Donkey in *Shrek?*
5. Helen Parr in *The Incredibles?*
6. Mike Wazowski in *Monsters, Inc.?*
7. Mrs. Potts in *Beauty and the Beast?*
8. Woody in *Toy Story?*
9. Scar in *The Lion King?*
10. The Genie in *Aladdin?*

I Know That Voice! Answers

1. Jerry Orbach
2. Peggy Lee
3. Bob Newhart
4. Eddie Murphy
5. Holly Hunter
6. Billy Crystal
7. Angela Lansbury
8. Tom Hanks
9. Jeremy Irons
10. Robin Williams

Chapter 6
And the Award Goes To ...

Chapter Objective

Students will learn about the different acting awards available currently to actors and actresses. They will use creative skills to create a new awards show and trophy.

Activity Overview

The MTV Movie Awards have been called the "Oscars for the youth." Other groups have jumped onboard with awards shows aimed at younger audiences (i.e., Teen Choice Awards). Have the students design a new awards show for people their age. In addition, design the actual award/trophy to be presented.

Items to consider: What categories will be included? Think about your target audience. It might help to know that these are the current award categories for the MTV Movie Awards: Best Movie, Best Performance (usually separated into male and female categories), Best Breakthrough Performance (sometimes separated into male and female categories), Best Cast, Best On-Screen Dirtbag, Best Gut-Wrenching Performance, Best Comedic Performance, Best Music, Best Kiss, Best Fight, Best Hero.

Get into the details and plan out your show's theme. Who will be the emcee? What types of entertainment will you have? How do your actors get nominated? Will schools across the nation vote? What does the award look like? Did you know that the MTV Movie Award looks like a bucket of popcorn? Or that the Teen Choice Award is an authentic full-size surfboard? Create a prototype of a trophy that would appeal to students your own age!

Project Timeline

Use one class period to teach students about the different awards shows currently being offered for actors and actresses. Designing an awards show and trophy can take several class periods, best done in groups of three or four. Use another class period or two to have each group do a presentation to the class revealing their award concept and trophy design.

Awards Shows

Academy Awards: Each January, the entertainment community and film fans around the world turn their attention to the Academy Awards. Interest and anticipation build to a fevered pitch, leading up to the Oscar telecast in February when hundreds of millions of movie lovers tune in to watch the glamorous ceremony to learn who will receive the highest honors in filmmaking.

The Oscars reward the previous year's greatest cinematic achievements as determined by some of the world's most accomplished motion picture artists and professionals. The Academy's roughly six thousand members vote for the Oscars using secret ballots, which are tabulated by the international auditing firm of PricewaterhouseCoopers. The auditors maintain absolute secrecy until the moment the show's presenters open the envelopes and reveal the winners on live television.

Teen Choice Awards: The Teen Choice Awards is an annual awards show that airs on the Fox Network. The awards honor the year's biggest achievements in music, movies, sports, television, fashion, and more, voted by teen viewers aged fourteen through seventeen. Winners receive an authentic full-size surfboard designed with the graphics of that year's show.

Check out their site at www.teenchoiceawards.com.

Golden Globe Awards: The Hollywood Foreign Press Association's annual Golden Globe Awards have enabled the non-profit organization to donate more than $12 million in the past seventeen years to entertainment-related charities, as well as funding scholarships and other programs for future film and television professionals. In the year 2011, the donation was a record $1,579,500, the largest tally ever distributed in the organization's history.

Known worldwide for its glittering Golden Globe Awards ceremony held every January and its multi-million dollar donations to charity, the Hollywood Foreign Press Association had humble origins that stemmed solely from a group of journalists' desire to efficiently and accurately cover all aspects of the world of entertainment according to GoldenGlobes.org.

Screen Actors Guild Awards: Lauded by critics for its style, simplicity, and genuine warmth, the Screen Actors Guild Awards, which made its debut in 1995, has become one of the industry's most prized honors. The only televised awards show to exclusively honor performers, it presents thirteen awards for acting in film and television in a fast-moving, two-hour show which airs live on TNT and TBS. The awards focus on both individual performances as well as on the work of the entire ensemble of a drama series and comedy series and the cast of a motion picture. These honors are fundamental to the spirit of the Screen Actors Guild Awards because they recognize what all actors know — that acting is a collaborative art. Check out their website at www.sagawards.org.

BET Awards: The BET Awards were established in 2001 by the Black Entertainment Television network to celebrate African Americans and other minorities in music, acting, sports, and other fields of entertainment over the past year. The awards are presented annually and broadcast live on BET. Check out their website at www.bet.com.

MTV Movie Awards: The MTV Movie Awards is a film awards show presented annually on MTV. The nominees are decided by producers and executives at MTV. Winners are decided online by the general public. Presently voting is done through MTV's official website through a special movie awards link at www.movieawards.mtv.com.

Variations of Idea or Add-Ons

✎ If timed right, have students watch a live show and record the winners of specified categories, or research winners online in class or in the computer lab.

✎ Instead of creating an actor/movie awards show, have students create an awards show for their school. If they were in charge of those boring, end-of-school-year award presentations, what would they do differently? What would be the categories for nominations, and how would students be selected? Would teachers have a vote, or just the students?

✎ Have students lobby for their favorite actor by writing a summary as to why he/she should win "Best Actor of the Year."

✎ Have students write an acceptance speech for the award they would most like to receive and then perform it for the class. Encourage them to be overdramatic in their acceptance speech to make it more entertaining.

✎ Act out an awards show — fancy dresses, suits, and all. Decorate the room with a "red carpet" and give students a chance to see what their future might hold. Have them present their memorable acceptance speeches! I found all kinds of Hollywood-type decorations at the dollar store.

Tips & Tricks

- If the project is too big, pick one aspect, such as the trophy design, and skip the rest. Or list out the specific things you're looking for to help guide the students. For example, categories of nomination, how actors will be nominated, show outline, or trophy design.
- You can make a trophy out of just about anything. Think creatively. How can an ordinary item represent what your awards show is all about?
- The key to designing an awards show is determining what's important to you. Maybe you want to focus on animated movies only. Or comedians. Or those who perform charitable work. Find a theme that interests you and go with it!

Fun Facts

- MTV Movie awards are creative and aimed at younger audiences. Here's a list of former awards:
  Most Desirable Male (1992–1996)
  Most Desirable Female (1992–1996)
  Best Action Sequence (1992–2005)
  Best New Filmmaker (1992–2002)
  Best Dance Sequence (1995, 1998, 2001, 2004)
  Best Sandwich in a Movie (1996)
  Best Cameo (2001–2002, 2004)
  Best Dressed (2001–2002)
  Best Virtual Performance (2003)
  Best Video Game Based on a Movie (2005)
  Sexiest Performance (2006)
  Best Summer Movie You Haven't Seen Yet (2007)
  Best Summer Movie So Far (2008)
  Global Superstar (2010)
  Best Line From a Movie (2011)

- According to Forbes.com, Oscar winners don't really own their statues. Winners must sign an agreement stating that should they wish to sell their statuettes, they must first offer them to the Academy for one dollar. If the winners refuse, they cannot keep their trophy. The rule has been in effect since 1950, which means that older statues do sometimes appear on the open market. In 1999, Michael Jackson paid $1.5 million dollars for the 1939 Best Picture Oscar for *Gone with the Wind.*

- The three movies that won the most Oscars were *Lord of the Rings: Return of the King* (2003), *Titanic* (1997), and *Ben-Hur* (1959). Each of those movies won eleven statuettes.
- In the past, people have purchased scalped tickets to the Oscars for as much as $30,000 to $40,000.

Chapter 7
You Expect Me to Memorize That?

Chapter Objective

Memorization is key to being a successful actor. Oftentimes, actors are given very little time to memorize a scene. In these activities, students will realize the importance of finding an approach that suits them best and practicing their memorization skills.

Activity Overview

First, have students write down ten random objects and number them one through ten. Now give them ten minutes to memorize the list by making up a story using the items in order on the list they just created. They will write the story down as they create it. They will then recite their story to the class while the teacher holds the list to see if they get them in order. For example: My first three items are milk, pencil, and couch. I might say something like, "I was drinking a glass of milk at the table when my brother threw a pencil at my head, so I tackled him to the couch."

Project Timeline

This project is quick and easy and can be done in one class period. You can decide to do other variations during additional class time if desired.

Variations of Idea or Add-Ons

✎ Memorize the little things: Set out a table full of twenty items or so, and as students are coming in to class, instruct them to spend a few moments looking at the table. Tell them that you will be discussing the items in class later. Once everyone has had a chance to view the items, remove them from a table to where they cannot be seen any longer. Begin the class as normal. After approximately fifteen minutes, have them take out a piece of paper and write down as many of the items as they can remember. Offer a small prize to whoever remembers the most. *Note:* Don't have time to round up twenty random items? Create a PowerPoint slide of items using pictures or clip art instead!

✎ Play the "alphabet game," but the letters have to stand for something drama-related. (i.e., a − actor, b − boom, c − camera, etc.)

✎ Have each student share their favorite line from a movie. Then, have the class name the movie.

✎ Have students complete the "Movie Quotes" activity on page 40. You could also have students create their own movie quote worksheet for the class to complete.

Tips & Tricks

- Read your lines out loud, over and over and over again.
- Record your lines and then listen to them over and over. Think about how fast you learn the lyrics to a song on the radio. It's because you hear it many times without even realizing you're listening.
- Record the scene using your phone, video recorder, MP3 player, etc. and watch/listen to it over and over. (Are you getting the picture yet? *Over and over* is key!)
- Don't break character if you do forget a line. It's going to happen! Most times, no one but you will ever know — as long as you stay in character and keep the flow moving!
- Add it on! Read the first line. Then say it without looking at the script. Read the next line. Say the first two lines without looking at the script. Keep repeating until you've memorized all of your lines. You'll know you've got it when you can repeat the entire thing at least three times without peeking at the script!
- If your line has a series of items in it (i.e., "But I love him, Mom. He's smart, cute, funny, caring, and he loves me, too!"), make up an acronym using the first letter or two of each word so that you can keep them in order (i.e., S, CU, F, CA could be "Scientist Cure For Cancer").
- Use flash cards. Put your prompts on one side and your lines on another. Pull from the prompt pile and say the line that follows the

prompt. Once you get it down that way, switch and pull from the line pile. (It's harder to do it in the reverse!)
- Say your lines to someone or in front of a mirror.
- Some people are visual learners. It may help to write out or type out your lines multiple times.
- Over-exaggerate your lines while you're practicing them alone. This will leave a bigger imprint on your brain/memory.

Fun Facts

Most memorable lines from Disney animated movies:
- Magic Mirror on the wall, who is the fairest one of all?" *(Snow White)*
- "A lie keeps growing and growing until it's as plain as the nose on your face." *(Pinocchio)*
- "Hakuna Matata. It means 'no worries.'" *(The Lion King)*
- "Ten thousand years will give you such a crick in the neck." *(Aladdin)*
- "Your mother can't be with you anymore." *(Bambi)*

Actors aren't the only ones who sometimes make mistakes (like messing up a line you definitely had memorized!). Check out these movie bloopers:
- From *Pirates of the Caribbean: The Curse of the Black Pearl,* just as Jack says, "On deck, you scabrous dogs," on the very left edge of the screen over Jack's shoulder is a grip crew member with a tan cowboy hat, white short-sleeved t-shirt, and sunglasses, just standing there looking out to sea.
- From *The Twilight Saga: Eclipse,* in the last scene where Edward and Bella are sitting in the sunny field, Edward is not sparkling.
- From *Spider-Man,* when Peter shoots his web at his bedroom lamp and pulls it across the room, it smashes against the wall and breaks. But when Aunt May is talking to Peter from the door seconds later, the lamp is back on the dresser in one piece.
- From *The Lord of the Rings: The Two Towers,* Merry and Pippin were bound when taken by the Uruk-hai, and the bonds weren't cut until after they managed to escape during the fight. Yet, when the horse almost crashed down on Pippin, he had his arms spread out up near his face, not bound, even though they weren't cut until later. In the next shot, his hands are bound again.

- From *Beauty and the Beast,* in the Gaston song sequence near the end, Gaston is sitting in his huge antler chair with Lefou. In the wide shot, there is a bear rug behind the chair. The camera does a close up of Gaston, then in the next wide shot, the chair is on top of the bear rug. Also, after this, Gaston gets up off of the chair and in the next shot, both the chair and the rug disappear completely.
- From *Grease,* in the soda shop, the waitress turns off the lights with her elbow because her hands are full, but she misses the light switch by six inches.

Movie Quotes

Finish off these famous quotes and then list the movie it came from:

1. "I see _____ people." _____

2. " _____ Johnny." _____

3. " _____, we have a problem." _____

4. "And in the morning, I'm making _____." _____

5. "There's no place like _____." _____

6. "I'm king of the _____." _____

7. "Mama always said life was like a box of _____." _____

8. "You're gonna need a bigger _____." _____

9. " _____ means family, family means nobody gets left behind. Or forgotten." _____

10. "The past can hurt. But the way I see it, you can either run from it or _____ from it." _____

Movie Quotes Answers

1. dead; *The Sixth Sense*
2. Heeeere's; *The Shining*
3. Houston; *Apollo 13*
4. waffles; *Shrek*
5. home; *The Wizard of Oz*
6. world; *Titanic*
7. chocolates; *Forrest Gump*
8. boat; *Jaws*
9. Ohana; *Lilo and Stitch*
10. learn; *The Lion King*

Chapter 8

You Gotta See This!

Chapter Objective

Students will use creative-thinking skills to add a twist to a classic story, basically a modern-day take on a classic fairy tale. This is a popular technique in bringing a classic or famous character back to life into the movie theater, Broadway, or high school gymnasium!

Who would have ever guessed that a story about Abraham Lincoln could actually be about vampires? *Abraham Lincoln: Vampire Hunter* (2012). Another classic tale with a twist is *Jack the Giant Killer* (2012). The story follows the traditional lines of Jack who accidently grows a giant beanstalk, but this is where the story differs. This time the house was taken up into the sky when the beanstalk grew. Somehow the princess was in the house and is now at the top of the beanstalk where she has been taken captive by a giant. Jack must rescue the princess and defeat the giant.

Activity Overview

Your school has decided to perform the classic *Cinderella*. But to get students to attend, it needs a twist. Design a marketing campaign/poster around a new twist to the classic fairy tale that will get students talking!

Project Timeline

This can be done in one or two class periods depending on how long students need for brainstorming and designing the poster, flyer, etc. If students write a scene for their proposed *Cinderella* adaptation, add a few more class periods to the project.

Variations of Idea or Add-Ons

✎ Let the class pick their own classic instead of having everyone do a version of *Cinderella*.

✎ Have students perform a monologue from the book, *Famous Fantasy Character Monologs*. Students will reveal a side of each character that no one's ever seen before!

✎ Have students work in groups to create a scene from their newly adapted *Cinderella* play.

✎ From the "Fun Facts" section, have students read one of the books that became a movie and then watch the movie in class and make a list/synopsis of how the book differed from the movie. (Either you pick or have the class vote.)

✎ You're a little sketchy: Each student needs a pen or pencil and a piece of paper. They start by writing down the name of a movie at the top of the sheet. Then everyone passes their sheet of paper to the person on their left. Everyone draws a sketch of the title that appears on the sheet that they have just received. When this is done, they fold over the paper so that the title is concealed and only the sketch is visible. Everyone passes their sheet of paper to the left again. Now players have to guess the title depicted by the sketch just received and write their guess below the sketch. Then fold over the paper so that the sketch is concealed and only the text is visible. This continues until everyone reaches the bottom of the sheets. Once the sheet is done, open it up and share with the class. If you find that people are taking too long over the sketches, impose a time limit. Thirty seconds to one minute works best. Scoring is optional. If you choose to score them, make sure each student includes their initials beside each sketch or title they write. Award one point each time a student correctly guesses a sketch, and also give a point to the person who drew the sketch.

✎ You can't have a great play without an evil character! Have the students complete the "Evil Is as Evil Does" activity on page 46 for a refresher on famous evil characters.

Tips & Tricks

- You need to really think outside the box on this one! Nothing is too crazy to consider. After the book *Twilight* became a hit both in bookstores and at the movies, tons of other vampire books hit the shelves as well as television series. Maybe *Cinderella* doesn't need a vampire too, but could it be something just as unexpected?
- Do some research on other classic characters, comics, or fairy tales that have been given a revitalized twist. It may spur an idea!
- Think about what appeals to you. If you like it, chances are your classmates will, too!

Fun Facts

- The movie, *Abraham Lincoln: Vampire Hunter* (2012) takes a historical movie theme and makes it current. However, it had an underwhelming box office opening, only grossing $16.5 million. The average viewer only rated the movie a "C+."
- *Snow White and the Huntsman* (2012), another movie with a twist to a commonly known tale, grossed $56.3 million during its opening. Viewers rated this movie a "B."
- Novels are primarily internal, film is external. This is why oftentimes moviegoers are disappointed when books come alive on the big screen. Here are a few book-to-movie changes you may or may not have noticed:
  1. *Twilight:* In the book, Bella uses a CD player. In the movie, she uses an iPod. In the book, Bella has an old desktop computer. In the movie, Bella has a new Apple laptop. (Remember product placement?)
  2. *The Hunger Games:* In the movie, Katniss is given her famous mockingjay pin by a woman in the Hob and takes it home to give to Prim, her sister. Prim gives it back to Katniss during their emotional goodbye. It's a sweet moment that shows their love of one another. In the book, though, the pin was given to Katniss by another girl from District 12, Madge. Madge is the daughter of the mayor of District 12, and is one of Katniss' very few friends at school. She really doesn't play much of a role in the rest of the books, so it's no great loss to lose her in the movie.
  3. *The Wizard of Oz:* Many of the perils that Dorothy encountered in the book are not present in the movie. Dorothy had silver shoes originally in the book. In the original novel, Oz is meant to be a real place that Dorothy would return to later. In the movie, it was all just a dream.

    4. *Harry Potter and the Deathly Hallows:* In the movie, Peter
       Pettigrew doesn't die. In the book, Peter Pettigrew's magical
       metal hand turns against him when he hesitates for a
       moment before killing Harry.
    5. *The Lord of the Rings: Return of the King:* The character
       Beregond was completely left out of the movie.

- Academy Awards 2012: Six out of the nine Best Picture Academy
Award nominees were based on books: *Hugo, War Horse,
Moneyball, The Descendants, The Help,* and *Extremely Loud &
Incredibly Close.*
- Here are some movies that are based on some great books for kids
aged six to twelve:
  The Secret World of Arrietty (2012)
  Hugo (2012)
  Mr. Popper's Penguins (2011)
  Judy Moody and the Not Bummer Summer (2011)
  Charlotte's Web (2006)
  Charlie and the Chocolate Factory (2005)
  Hotel for Dogs (2009)
  Because of Winn Dixie (2005)
  How to Eat Fried Worms (2006)
  Arthur and the Invisibles (2006)
  The Spiderwick Chronicles (2008)
  Bridge to Terabithia (2007)
  Lemony Snicket's A Series of Unfortunate Events (2004)
  Ramona and Beezus (2010)
  *The Chronicles of Narnia: The Lion, the Witch,
  and the Wardrobe* (2005)
  Diary of a Wimpy Kid (2010)
  Dr. Seuss' The Lorax (2012)

Evil Is as Evil Does

Can you name the famous evil characters below?

1. This evil woman is mean to puppies.
2. This Bond villain has an underground lair, a giant laser beam, and is a member of the terrorist organization called SPECTRE.
3. This cannibal has an appetite for evil — literally.
4. This evil clown has some twisted makeup and a sick sense of humor.
5. He-Who-Must-Not-Be-Named. Enough said.
6. A corrupt politician from outer space. He has finger-lightning.
7. This evil little kid rides a Big Wheel around the house and tries to kill his adoptive mother.
8. This is one vampire Bella would *not* want to meet. He's the *real* original.
9. This dude's got some razor-sharp ends on his fingers.
10. This guy must be a fan of hockey.

Evil Is as Evil Does Answers

1. Cruella De Vil
2. Dr. No
3. Hannibal Lecter
4. The Joker
5. Voldemort
6. Emperor Palpatine
7. Damien
8. Count Dracula
9. Freddy Krueger
10. Jason Voorhees

Chapter 9
The Infamous Actor X Takes the Stage

Chapter Objective

The objective is to get students thinking about the kind of actor (or person in general) they would like to be and to design a creative symbol that represents who they are. This project utilizes creative thinking and artistic skills.

Activity Overview

Draw a symbol that represents you as an actor. In 1993, the artist known as Prince shocked the world by changing his name to simply a symbol, usually spelled out O(+>.

As artists or actors, it's important to know who you are. How many times have you heard the phrase "Know who you are" on *American Idol* when the judges are trying to figure out to which category/genre a certain singer should belong? For a publicity company to market you, they have to *know* you. What would represent the type of actor you want to be? Will it be something quirky and fun to represent comedy? Or something dark and tragic? Will you be sweet and innocent, the all-American girl or boy, or will you be more like Madonna, whose entire career seems to be about crossing the line?

Project Timeline

This project should only take one class period for creation but can take more class periods if you ask students to present their ideas and explain their selection.

Variations of Idea or Add-Ons

✎ Prince wasn't the first person to use a symbol instead of a name. Students may research others who preceded this famous artist.

✎ Art not their thing? Instead of a symbol, let students pick a word that represents them as an actor. Then ask the students to write a short summary explaining why they picked that word.

✎ Maybe they can't narrow it down to one thing. A collage is a great idea for showing multiple facets to a career or personality.

✎ Have students complete the "Catch Phrase" activity on page 50.

✎ Maybe developing a slogan works better for your students. Students may spend some time researching product, company, or service slogans. (Or you can just use the slogans in the activfity on page 51.) Each student should select a slogan that represents who they are or who they want to be. Write a paragraph summary explaining why the slogan represents them.

Tips & Tricks

- Put some thought into this. If you get famous, you'll want to be known for something. What will it be? Do you want to be like Howard Stern, radio personality, known as one of the first "shock jocks"? Or are you more like Angelina Jolie, known for her worldwide humanitarian efforts? Or maybe you want to be known as the funniest person in America, like Ellen DeGeneres (Showtime's Funniest Person in America, 1982).
- You don't have to be an artist to create a meaningful symbol. Simple is awesome — look at Prince's! Take a piece of clipart and make it your own by adding small details or coloring.

Fun Facts

- According to Wikipedia.org, Prince explained his name change as follows:
  "The first step I have taken toward the ultimate goal of emancipation from the chains that bind me to Warner Bros. was to change my name from Prince to the Love Symbol. Prince is the name that my mother gave me at birth. Warner Bros. took

the name, trademarked it, and used it as the main marketing tool to promote all of the music that I wrote. The company owns the name Prince and all related music marketed under Prince. I became merely a pawn used to produce more money for Warner Bros. ... I was born Prince and did not want to adopt another conventional name. The only acceptable replacement for my name, and my identity, was the Love Symbol, a symbol with no pronunciation that is a representation of me and what my music is about. This symbol is present in my work over the years; it is a concept that has evolved from my frustration; it is who I am. It is my name."

- Long before Prince became the "artist known by a symbol," English poets signed their work with a symbol. In fact, only two Old English poets are known by name, Cynewulf and Caedmon.
- According to DidYouKnow.org, the artist previously known as Prince was born Prince Rogers Nelson on June 7, 1958 in Minneapolis. On his thirty-fifth birthday, he announced that he would change his name to an unpronounceable symbol. The glyph incorporates the male and female signs along with the alchemy symbol for soapstone. In May 2000, he announced that he is again to be known as "Prince."

Catch Phrases

Do you know who said these famous catch phrases?

1. "How you doin'?"
2. "Just keep swimming."
3. "D'oh!"
4. "Aaay!"
5. "And that's the way it is."
6. "Don't make me angry."
7. "Good grief!"
8. "Is that your final answer?"
9. "Live long and prosper."
10. "The tribe has spoken."

Catch Phrases Answers

1. Joey, *Friends*
2. Dory, *Finding Nemo*
3. Homer, *The Simpsons*
4. Fonzie, *Happy Days*
5. Walter Kronkite, *CBS Evening News*
6. David Banner, *The Incredible Hulk*
7. Charlie Brown, *Peanuts*
8. Regis Philbin, *Who Wants to Be a Millionaire?*
9. Spock, *Star Trek*
10. Jeff Probst, *Survivor*

Hey, That's My Slogan!

1. It's the real thing.
2. Think Different
3. Impossible Is Nothing
4. Quality never goes out of style.
5. Something for Everyone
6. The Difference Is Clear
7. Think what we can do for you.
8. Sponsors of Tomorrow
9. Just slightly ahead of our time
10. Where do you want to go today?
11. Let's make things better.
12. Be all you can be.
13. Some of our best men are women.
14. Life's Good
15. Sharp Minds, Sharp Products
16. Because you're worth it.
17. When it absolutely, positively has to be there overnight.
18. We try harder.
19. I'm lovin' it.
20. The true definition of luxury. Yours.

Companies/Products to Choose From:

Avis Rental Cars, Sharp, Bank of America, McDonald's, Coca-Cola, 7-Up, Apple, Acura, L'Oréal, Levi's, Microsoft, Federal Express (FedEx), U.S. Army, Pepsi-Cola, Adidas, Intel, Philips, LG.

Hey, That's My Slogan! Answers

1. Coca-Cola
2. Apple
3. Adidas
4. Levi's
5. Pepsi-Cola
6. 7-Up
7. Bank of America
8. Intel
9. Panasonic
10. Microsoft
11. Philips
12. U.S. Army
13. U.S. Army
14. LG
15. Sharp
16. L'Oréal
17. Federal Express (FedEx)
18. Avis Rental Cars
19. McDonald's
20. Acura

Chapter 10
Rockin' Resume

Chapter Objective

It's time to once again get students thinking about the future and who they want to be. Only this time, they get to dream big — about their past! Were they discovered and whisked off to California to star in a new Disney series at the age of fifteen? Did they perform in any advertisements on television? Or a Broadway musical? What high school performances did they star in? Or maybe they were doing a two-bit part in the background and a Hollywood agent noticed their potential! Students will use their creative-thinking skills and imaginations to create a resume that anyone would dream of having.

Activity Overview

Prepare a resume that would represent who you are in the future. For example, what high school performances were you involved in? Were you discovered while shopping at the mall? Maybe you performed in some local television advertisements that went national? Or maybe you were an overnight YouTube sensation. Dream big. What can you accomplish by the time you're sixteen? Twenty? Will you star in a Disney television series? Be the next actress-gone-singer? Or vice versa?

Project Timeline

This project can take anywhere between one and three class periods depending on if you do an add-on, such as having the students perform as an announcer for their future self.

Variations of Idea or Add-Ons

✎   Once the resumes are complete, have students perform as an announcer for their future self. "And introducing ..."

✎ Teach students how to prepare a real acting resume. (See "Tips and Tricks" section on page 54.) There are many websites that offer free samples and templates for acting resumes.

✎ If you have access to digital cameras (or cell phones with cameras that can upload pictures to computers), have students create a headshot for their fake portfolio/resume.

✎ Pick your favorite actor. Research and write their real acting resume.

✎ Let students complete the "What Made Them Famous?" activity on page 56 during class as teams or as an individual assignment.

✎ In groups, have students create their own *Jeopardy!* game about actors and the movies or shows that made them famous. The "What Made Them Famous?" activity is about actors who started out as child stars. But every actor has to have a beginning and a show that helped them become famous. Make it fun to learn the history of famous celebrities! (Chapter 16, starting on page 83, is all about games.)

Tips & Tricks

- Acting headshots are usually eight by ten inches and are used as a quick identification of the person — so make sure yours looks like you. This isn't the time to add fancy backgrounds or make silly faces. They are typically very neutral. A headshot should portray you in the best possible light. (Modeling headshots, on the other hand, are more like beauty shots.)
- When you're writing your real acting resume, you'll have to stick to the facts. According to Actorspages.org, here are a few resume "dos and don'ts:"

"Dos:"

- Print or staple your resume to the back of your headshot. Use only one staple in the upper left corner.
- If you are stapling, trim your resume to fit the headshot. Cut your resume to eight by ten inches.
- Make sure the contact information on the back is up-to-date and you have an email address.
- If you have a lot of projects, it's better to list the best ones.

"Don'ts:"
- Never lie about your experience.
- Don't make up special skills or write things down just to fill in the special skills area.
- Don't use paper that is larger than eight and a half by eleven inches.
- Don't use a resume that is more than one page.
- Don't staple reviews or clippings to your resume. They just get in the way.
- Don't make the type smaller than ten point font. If you have that much experience, edit it down.

Fun Facts

- Sylvester Stallone was a struggling actor with very little money when he wrote the rough draft of the *Rocky* script — in just three days! He was inspired after watching Muhammad Ali fight Chuck Wepner. Against all odds, Wepner survived fifteen rounds against the legend.
- Hilary Swank and her mother lived in a car for a while when Swank was pursuing her acting career in California.
- John Grisham's first book was rejected at twelve publishing houses and by sixteen agents.
- A producer told Marilyn Monroe that she was unattractive and couldn't act.
- Julia Roberts auditioned for the soap opera show *All My Children* and got rejected.
- Oprah was fired from a job as a television reporter because she was "unfit for TV."
- Drama instructors told Lucille Ball to try another profession.
- Harrison Ford was once told by movie executives that he simply didn't have what it takes to be a star.
- Steven Spielberg was rejected from the University of Southern California School of Theater, Film, and Television three times.
- Michael Jordan was actually cut from his high school basketball team.

What Made Them Famous?

Can you name the movie or television show for which the then-child star listed below is most famous? (Their claim to fame.)

1. Macaulay Culkin
2. Jonathan Lipnicki
3. Keisha Knight Pulliam
4. Sarah Jessica Parker
5. Dakota Fanning
6. Mary-Kate and Ashley Olsen
7. Drew Barrymore
8. Christina Ricci
9. Elijah Wood
10. Raven-Symoné
11. Neil Patrick Harris
12. Ron Howard
13. Lindsay Lohan
14. Christian Bale
15. Kirsten Dunst
16. Britney Spears
17. Jodie Sweetin
18. Vanessa Hudgens
19. Haley Joel Osment
20. Jessica Biel

What Made Them Famous Answers

1. *Home Alone*
2. *Jerry Maguire* and *Stuart Little*
3. *The Cosby Show*
4. *Square Pegs*
5. *I Am Sam*
6. *Full House*
7. *E.T.*
8. *The Addams Family*
9. *Back to the Future II*
10. *The Cosby Show*
11. *Doogie Howser, M.D.*
12. *The Andy Griffith Show*
13. *The Parent Trap*
14. *Empire of the Sun*
15. *Interview with the Vampire*
16. *The New Mickey Mouse Club*
17. *Full House*
18. *High School Musical*
19. *The Sixth Sense*
20. *7th Heaven*

Chapter 11

It's All about Character

Chapter Objective

To become a character, you must know the character. Inside and out. The objective is to get students thinking more about what's on the inside of a character than the outside.

Activity Overview

Students will "interview" a character based on a random photograph that either the teacher provides or they find in a magazine.

Why? Authors often talk about how their characters speak to them or take directions in a story that they never saw coming. It's because they allowed themselves to think freely and allowed the character to "drive the bus," so to speak. Don't be afraid to let your character take you somewhere.

A writer once told me that she often sat down to "talk" to the little girl in her book. Honestly, as a new writer at the time, I thought she was crazy! Did she really "see" this little girl from her manuscript? I imagined a sort of weird empty-chair-tea-party kind of thing going on. But after attending other workshops that really focused on character development, I finally got it! When you "interview" your character, you find out all kinds of things. Details that don't always show up in your story, but help shape your character into who he or she is!

Project Timeline

This project should only take one to two class periods.

Variations of Idea or Add-Ons

✎ Instead of a random picture of a person, choose a character from a well-known book (such as a fairy tale, or maybe even a comic book) and interview that character.

✎ Instead of using the activity at the end of the chapter ("Character Interview: Things You Should Know about Your Character" found on page 60), have students create their own list of questions that they would like to ask.

✎ Once the students have developed an in-depth character, have them write a scene with that character. It could be fun to do this assignment in groups at this point, where they would have to find a reason to intertwine their characters with other's characters. They may also perform the scene.

Tips & Tricks

- It may sound crazy, but really try to picture your character talking to you. If you can see and hear them, you'll understand them better!
- Go beyond his or her appearance. Why does the character look the way they do? Everyone has a story. What is theirs?
- Characters do things. Characters think things. Characters speak about things. Characters feel things. *Think* about your character. Now *think* again. If your character doesn't feel real to you, it won't feel real to your audience.
- Ask your character to "take you somewhere." Now ask them why they took you there.
- Be careful when naming your character. First, make sure it is a name that others can pronounce, unless the fact that it is hard to pronounce is a part of your character's back story. Avoid common names that are easily forgotten. Lastly, you may want to choose a name based on the meaning of the name, but maybe with a twist. For example, name an old witchy woman Belle, which means beautiful. That's something people will remember.

Fun Facts

- Hank Azaria provides many of the voices for *The Simpsons*.
- A distinctive voice or accent may limit roles for which an actor can audition. Can you automatically "hear" the voice of these famous actors:
   James Earl Jones (voiceover: Mufasa — *The Lion King)*
   Gilbert Gottfried (voiceover: Iago — *Aladdin)*
   Julie Kavner (voiceover: Marge Simpson — *The Simpsons)*
   Vin Diesel (voiceover: the *Iron Giant)*
   Fergie (voiceover: Charlie Brown's little sister, Sally — *Peanuts)*
   Howie Mandel (Gizmo — *Gremlins)*

• Here are a few memorable names from movies: (Maybe you can name the movie or show associated with the character.)

Ethan Hunt — *Mission Impossible*

Indiana Jones —Indiana Jones movies (i.e., *Indiana Jones and the Raiders of the Lost Ark*)

Jerry Maguire — *Jerry Maguire*

Rocky Balboa — *Rocky*

Pepper Potts — *Iron Man*

Captain Jack Sparrow — Pirates of the Caribbean movies (i.e., *Pirates of the Caribbean: The Curse of the Black Pearl*)

Gilbert Grape — *What's Eating Gilbert Grape*

Scarlett O'Hara — *Gone with the Wind*

James Bond — James Bond movies (i.e., *Dr. No*)

Character Interview:
Things You Should Know about Your Character

1. Look in the mirror and tell me what you see.
2. You just realized you have a hole in your pocket and you're really upset. Why? What fell out of it?
3. Do you have brothers and sisters, or are you an only child?
4. You're mad at your brother, sister, or best friend. Why?
5. You have a picture beside your bed. What is in the picture?
6. What is on your bed? What type of blankets and pillows? Are they new, old, handmade?
7. Describe your favorite outfit. Why do you like it so much?
8. You recently attended a funeral. Who died? How did you feel?
9. What are you going to do today?
10. Name the most unusual thing in your closet.
11. Who's your best friend? Why?
12. You just found a twenty-dollar bill on the ground. What will you do with it?
13. What kind of family do you have? Do you live with your parents? One parent? Grandparents? Etc.
14. Whom do you like better: your mom or your dad? Why?
15. You have something in your pocket. What is it? Why?

Chapter 12
Masks & Movement

Chapter Objective

Students will learn the importance of body language in acting. To really emphasize the importance of non-verbal communication, students will hide behind masks that they create for this activity. (Some students may actually come out of their shell more since their faces will be hidden.)

Activity Overview

Students will create a mask to represent a character that they have designed. Then, students will develop a list of body movements that represent their character. If time allows, students can demonstrate how their character moves/acts in front of the class. Give instructions on how to create different masks. Use the information provided on pages 64-65.

Project Timeline

This project can take multiple class periods to allow time for designing the character, making the masks, and class demonstrations.

Variations of Idea or Add-Ons

✎ Spend a class period learning about the importance of body language. Especially when an actor is wearing a mask, body movements speak volumes. Ask students, how can your character stand out? What quirky movements would make them unique? Is your character apt to use large dramatic movements or quiet, shy gestures?

✎ Have students complete the "Body Language and Gestures" exercise on page 66.

✎ Facial expressions are huge when it comes to body language. Have students play this "Expressions" game as a warm-up activity: Have each student write two or three emotions on scraps of paper. (Angry, sad, confused, irritated, distraught, pensive, ashamed, etc.) You may want to mention that less "extreme" emotions will be the hardest to guess. You want your actors to be challenged! Collect the emotions into a hat or basket. Then, students will draw out one of the emotions and, without making any sounds, perform the emotion using only their face. The rest of the class will guess the emotion. *Note:* This can be done in small groups instead of with the whole class if desired.

✎ Play the "Movement" game: Stand in a circle so every actor is facing each other. One at a time, each actor should create a spontaneous movement that lasts one to two seconds. This movement may (or you can say it should) involve the entire body, and it does not require the actor to stay in place. Do not incorporate sound with the movement. The person next to the actor making the movement must then imitate those movements before creating a new movement that will be passed on to the person next to him/her. Continue through the whole group, adding a new movement each time.

✎ Play the "Mirror" game: Put the students into pairs. Tell them they are to pretend that they are each other's mirror and that they are to mimic what the other person is doing. If desired, have a pair of students demonstrate what they are to do for the class before letting the whole class begin the activity. Depending on time, suggest that the students switch partners to gain more practice.

✎ Have students write and perform a silent skit.

✎ Watch part of a show with the sound off and make note of the body movements and gestures of the actors. Can you tell what's going on?

✎ Play a good old-fashioned game of charades.

Tips & Tricks

- Practice reading your script (saying your lines) in the mirror while paying close attention to your facial expressions.
- Think about age-related body movements. What will you need to do differently if your character is very young or very old?
- Go somewhere where you can observe someone's movements and then try to mimic them.
- Practice making different faces in the mirror.
- During a class or group gathering, make notes of all the body movements you observe.
- Try holding a conversation with a friend or classmate without using *any* body movements.

Fun Facts

- Famous movie masks:
  - Leatherface — *The Texas Chainsaw Massacre*
  - Guy Fawkes mask — *V for Vendetta*
  - Robin's mask — *Batman*
  - Ghostface — *Scream*
  - Darth Vader — *Star Wars* series
  - Michael Myers mask — *Halloween*
  - Loki mask — *The Mask*
  - Opera mask — *The Phantom of the Opera*
  - Maximus' helmet — *Gladiator*
  - Predator mask — *Predator*
  - Zorro's mask — *Zorro* series
  - Hannibal Lecter's mask (muzzle) — *The Silence of the Lambs*
  - Batman's cowl — *Batman* series
  - Jason's hockey mask — *Friday the 13th* series
  - Spiderman's mask — *Spiderman* series
  - Dr. Doom's mask — *The Fantastic Four*
  - Tony Stark's Iron Man helmet — *Iron Man*

- Kristen Stewart, *The Twilight Saga,* has been dubbed by many as the actress with only one facial expression. Several websites have made spoof posters showing the "many expressions" of Kristen Stewart. Funny thing is … they are all the same!
- The movie *Mask* (1985) starring Cher won the Academy Award for Best Makeup. Cher also received a Golden Globe nomination for her performance. The movie was based on the life of a boy who suffered from disfiguring cranial enlargements known commonly as lionitis.

How to Make a Paper Mache Mask

According to the eHow.com article "How to Make Masks," mix water and white glue in a bowl. A three-to-one ratio of water to glue works best.

Build the basic structure of the mask. You can either use a balloon blown up to the appropriate size, or you can use strips of cardboard and/or cardboard tubes and then tape them together to form a rough mold of a head.

Use strips of newspaper to build up the basic mask. Tear off strips about two inches and then wet them. Dip your fingers into the adhesive and smooth the glue onto the strips.

Once you have a uniform covering of the mask, start making facial features. A great method to make eyebrows, lips, eye sockets, and other features is to ball up pieces of newspaper, dip them in the glue, and then secure them to the mask. Then, cover them in layer after layer of paper mache strips until you have the feature you want.

Make larger features out of cardboard and paper mache. For example, if you are making a nose, cut out several triangular pieces of cardboard in decreasing sizes and tape them one on top of the other. Then, cover the whole thing in paper mache and shape the nostrils using the method in step four. Finally, use strips of paper mache to join the nose to the rest of the mask.

Give the mask a chance to dry. You can simply leave it sitting or use a hair dryer or hot oven to speed up the process. Drying time will vary depending on the size of the mask.

Paint the mask. Pretty much any paint will work, but most people like to use cheap, water-based acrylic paints.

Use duct tape to secure heavy features if needed. Use several layers of paper mache to smooth over the joint.

Tin Foil and Tape Mask

According to the WikiHow.com article "How to Make a Mask out of Tin Foil and Tape," overlap three sheets aluminum foil in a stack.

Push the sheets at the same time onto your face. Push down as hard as you are comfortable pushing. Do it carefully, so the foil does not become punctured.

Make sure you have the general outline of your face: nose, lips, corners of your eyes, and cheekbones. Use a marker and trace around your eyes or have someone do it for you (it might be good to follow the bones around your eye socket) for where you want the eye holes in your mask to be. Also, trace around your lips for an air hole.

Carefully remove the foil from your face. Cut with sharp scissors around where you want the edges of the mask to be.

Carefully cut out the eye holes either by puncturing the foil with a toothpick and tearing the foil out, or snipping in the center of the area with the tip of scissors and folding the foil back.

Cut holes/slots in the side of your mask for the ribbons/cord/shoelaces to attach it to your face.

Cut small sections of masking tape, and, while pressing the mask to your face to keep the features strong, gently place the tape onto your mask. When you feel the mask's features are firm enough, place all the sections of tape, overlapping, across all visible places of foil, including the back, so the foil doesn't irritate your face. Or you can use packing tape if you want your mask to look crinkly and metallic.

If you want to add on any features (horns, a pointed nose, or antlers), just mold them out of foil and tape/glue them onto the mask.

Tie string, ribbon, shoelaces, etc. to the holes in the side of your mask, making sure to have enough length to not only wrap around your head, but also to tie in a knot or bow.

Use acrylic paints. Sprinkle glitter on the paint while it's wet if you like. Add sequins, feathers, beads, etc. if desired.

Other Mask Ideas

You can make a mask out of a ...

> Gourd
> Piece of cardboard
> Milk jug
> Paper bag
> Paper plate

Ordinary things you can use as "add-ons" to your mask:
(Just about anything, really!)

> Old CDs
> Yarn
> Feathers
> Buttons
> Sequins
> Sticks
> Sand
> Rocks
> Pipe cleaners
> Construction paper

Thread spools
Paperclips
Hair bows

Body Language and Gestures

How do you say the items listed below without using words and *only* using body movements/gestures? Describe in detail the position of your body or the gesture.

1. I'm OK.
2. Whatever.
3. I am so angry!
4. Wish me luck!
5. He's crazy!
6. We won!
7. Can I catch a ride?
8. I could use some money.
9. Call me.
10. You can't make me!

Body Language and Gestures Answers

Note: Answers may vary from those listed below and still be considered correct. Use student responses as a basis for discussion.

1. Thumb and forefinger connected in a circle while holding the other fingers straight.
2. Shoulders shrugged up and down.
3. Clenched fist.
4. Fingers crossed.
5. Pointer finger makes a circle movement around the ear.
6. Fist pump, closed fist raised up and down.
7. Sticking one thumb upward while rest of hand is clenched (hitchhiking sign).
8. Thumb rubbed repeatedly over the tip of the index finger and middle finger.
9. Thumb and pinky outstretched with other fingers tight against palm. Thumb to ear and pinky to mouth, as though they were a telephone receiver.
10. Hands on hips.

Chapter 13
I'm Not Playing, Bill!
Playbills That Grab You

Chapter Objective
Students will learn about the components of a playbill. They will use creative skills to create their own unique playbill.

Activity Overview
Have students create a playbill to help them understand all the components that go into a production, as well as get a taste for marketing. Assign each student or group an existing play (or book that could be made into a play), and then have them create the following: (For other possible items to include, see the "Tips and Tricks" section on page 69.)

- Playbill cover should reflect the name of the play and either a visual or a verbal "hook" to entice the viewer.
- Character descriptions for the main characters and supporting characters. Fake character names — what famous celebrity, or unknown, is going to star in the production?
- List of scenes.
- Other sections as desired: Thank yous, autographs, set design, advertisements, etc. (See "Tips and Tricks" section for more ideas.)

Project Timeline
This project can take several class periods for creative planning and creation of the playbill. This project can be done individually or in groups.

Variations of Idea or Add-Ons

✎ Spend the first class period showing students various playbills. Hopefully you've got a few to share. If not, print some from the Internet, or you can buy playbills at http://www.playbillstore.com/playbills.html. Go over the common components of a playbill. Also discuss which ones are the most effective. Based on the playbill, which plays would the students actually want to see?

✎ Have the students write a paper explaining their creative concept for the playbill.

✎ Some playbills include costume descriptions. Instead of a description of the costumes, students can create their own visuals by either drawing or cutting and pasting from magazines or Internet sites.

✎ Have students create a section for "fake" reviews from critics. What are those pesky critics saying about the production?

✎ Instead of a playbill booklet, make a playbill poster. Determine the most important information that must be included in this one-page format.

Tips & Tricks

- Information you may want to include:
  Who plays which character
  Who needs to be thanked
  Who directed the play
  Who wrote the play
  Who wrote the music (If it applies)
  Who directed the orchestra (If it applies)
  When and where are the performances

- All plays have themes. Figuring out the theme of your play will help you determine the design.
- Keep it simple. You can use just four pages of design on one piece of paper. The front and back covers on one side, which will be the outside of the playbill, and the inside of the playbill, which will list cast, scenes, thank yous, advertising, etc.
- Do you want to include a section for autographs? A lot of people like to ask actors to sign their playbill.

Fun Facts

- Originally staged as a mix of bold, chilling scenes at a 1980s high-school camp, *Carrie* closed on Broadway May 15, 1988 at the Virginia Theatre after only five regular performances. It was the most expensive flop in Broadway history, losing nearly $8 million.

- *The Phantom of the Opera* opened January 26, 1988, has approximately 10,000 performances, and is still running. It is the longest running musical in Broadway history.

- In 1998, *The Lion King* (Broadway musical) won six Tony Awards, including Best Musical, and eight Drama Desk Awards, and in 1999, it won a Grammy Award for Best Musical Show Album.

- The musical *Wicked* opened in 2003 and has won three Tony Awards. (I've seen this one three times already! It's amazing!) *Wicked* is the untold musical story of *The Wizard of Oz's* Wicked Witch of the West, Elphaba, and the Good Witch, Glinda, prior to the Dorothy years. The musical is loosely based on the best-selling novel *Wicked: The Life and Times of the Wicked Witch of the West* by Gregory Maguire.

- The television reality show *Grease: You're the One That I Want!* aired in January 2007. Winners of the show, Laura Osnes and Max Crumm, then starred in the Broadway production of *Grease.*

Here is a sample template of a playbill.

Fold

(Back cover)	(Cover)
Upcoming Performances: List dates, times, and locations of upcoming performances.	Title of Play
Acknowledgments or Autographs Who do you need to thank? List them here. Or use this section for autographs.	Written by: Directed by: Guest Appearance by:

Fold

Inside (page 2)	Inside (page 3)
Cast of Characters: Include character name, description, and actor name. Character Name Description Actor Name Dorothy Gale Farm Girl Judy Garland	**Setting:** Write a short description of the setting of each act or scene. Scene 1 Scene 2 Scene 3 Scene 4 Scene 5 **Reviews:** If you've seen the play, write a personal reaction. If not, make up a critique as if you are the reviewer.

Chapter 14
That Looks Like Something Your Grandma Would Wear

Chapter Objective

Students will learn about costume design by researching costumes used in other productions and by creating a design of their own.

Activity Overview

First have students research costumes used in a specific historical era. Then, students will design a costume for a current Broadway production or an original character that they design.

Project Timeline

This project can take several class periods for research and design. Add more class time if you have the students present their creations to the class.

Variations of Idea or Add-Ons

✎ Students can create their costume design on paper or by cutting items out of a magazine and pasting them onto a "paper doll" prototype.

✎ Have the students create real, life-size costumes and have them perform a fashion show or runway show.

✎ Have students create a scrapbook of their favorite costumes (from Broadway or movies).

✎ Have a specific "era" day and give students extra credit for dressing up. Students love making fun of the clothes their parents used to wear. And don't forget the hair. Who can forget the big-haired '80s!

✎ Gather photos of different clothing styles throughout the years and play a game show with the class (broken into two teams) to see who can name the historical period from which the costume/clothing came?

✎ Have students complete the "Costume Craziness" exercise on page 75.

Tips & Tricks

- You can find great items at thrift shops, yard sales, parents' or grandparents' closets, etc. (Maybe even those unclaimed items in the school lost and found box!)
- Many wallpaper stores will give you their old sample books for free. Wallpaper makes great "paper doll" clothes since it's more durable than plain old paper.
- Scrapbooking paper can be bought in bulk and has great color and design options.
- Old Halloween costumes can be altered into brand-new creations and can be inexpensively purchased right after the holiday.
- You don't have to be able to sew to create a costume idea. These don't have to be worn in a real production. Use glue, duct tape, double-sided tape, Velcro — whatever it takes! (All the beading for the costumes in *Wicked* was sewn on one bead at a time! No hot gluing for them!)
- Want to make a Jellicle cat costume from *Cats,* the musical, in five easy steps? According to Wikihow.com, you can!

   1. Create or buy a full-length jumpsuit. The jumpsuit should be made from a stretchy fabric like Lycra or jersey in a "cat color" such as silver, light brown, dark brown, ginger, or buy a plain white or black one. As an alternative, you can use a unitard (dance supply stores).
   2. Add the tail. A tail can be made very simply by stuffing newspaper into pantyhose and then gluing the fur pieces around it. Try to match the color of the pantyhose to the rest of the costume; visit a dollar store for extra pairs. Attach to the bodysuit part either by sewing, Velcro, or safety pin. You could also use yarn and tie a tail together.
   3. Create the headpiece. This is the part of the costume that will achieve the Jellicle cat look. Jellicle cats are more like lions in

their appearance, with fluffy manes surrounding the face. Ideas for making the headpiece include sewing a hood that joins directly with the bodysuit and adding fur and ears, sewing a separate hood that simply slips over the head and adding fur and ears, or creating a headpiece using non-sewing skills, such as using a basic flat hat with glue on the fur and ears. The fur should cascade around the face like a mane and create wispy pieces. Tease out the head fur with a comb to help achieve this effect. The head fur should match the body fur, although it can be a shade or two lighter.

4. Finish with the makeup. This part is very important and will distinguish you as a Jellicle cat. In particular, accent the eyes with cat-eye lines extending out to the side of your face.
5. Practice the Jellicle cat movements. Watch the DVD closely, mimicking the cat actions and singing the songs. When you wear the costume, these will bring it to life.

Tips for your Jellicle cat costume:
• Many costume stores will carry cat costumes that you could alter into a Jellicle cat. (Don't forget that *after* Halloween is a great time to stock up on cheap costumes!)
• You can wear a cat-style collar if you like. "Diamond"-studded or ribbon is nice. (You can buy these in stores, but they're pretty expensive!)
• When making the headpiece, remember that Jellicle cats don't really have very defined ears. You can make subtle ears by twisting some of the hair into the right shape (use glue or hair gel to hold them in place), or don't add them at all.

Fun Facts
• Bert Lahr, who played the Cowardly Lion in *The Wizard of Oz*, described the costume as hot and uncomfortable, like "working inside a mattress." The costume weighed ninety pounds and was made from two real lion skins.
• It takes 424 man hours per week to maintain the costumes for *Wicked* on Broadway.
• A yellow ellipse around the bat logo on Batman's chest was added in 1964 and became the hero's trademark symbol.
• The Phantom's makeup in *The Phantom of the Opera* takes two hours to put on and thirty minutes to take off.
• According to Anne Salt, the puppet supervisor who was part of the

original behind-the-scenes crew for *The Lion King,* there are over 250 masks and puppets used throughout the show. The giraffe puppets are eighteen feet tall!

- In October 2011, ABC news reported that the popular gaming character men's costume Halo 3 Master Chief Supreme Edition cost a whopping $800!

Costume Craziness

1. Marilyn Monroe is famous for her white dress. In what movie did she wear that dress?
2. One famous character wore a dress made from draperies. Who was it?
3. Black shorts, a man's vest, and a top hat along with stockings and high heels started a fashion outbreak. What famous actress wore this ensemble?
4. A white tuxedo shirt, red tie, sash, and black cape became a standard look for vampires. What movie started this trend?
5. What famous mom wears a bun wig and a raggedy gray dress? Hint: You definitely don't want her to be *your* mom.
6. Who wears a long-sleeved v-neck shirt with an attached black vest with pockets and navy pants with attached black boot covers? Hint: Another character from this movie is famous for his black mask.
7. White glove. Enough said.
8. This famous singer wore star-studded bell bottom pants. His hair was quite famous, too. Who is he?
9. This famous television housewife wore a blue polka-dotted dress with a white lace collar. You might need red hair if you're trying to be a copycat.
10. This first lady that made the pillbox hat a must-have for all women.

Costume Craziness Answers

1. *Seven Year Itch*
2. Scarlett (*Gone With the Wind*)
3. Liza Minnelli
4. *Dracula* (The original one)
5. Psycho Mom (From the movie *Psycho*)
6. Han Solo
7. Michael Jackson
8. Elvis
9. Lucille Ball
10. Jackie Kennedy

Chapter 15
Bet You Didn't Know That!

Chapter Objective

Students will research and learn about famous actors and celebrities (or movies and plays) while having some fun!

Activity Overview

Students will research funny or interesting facts about famous actors, movies, plays, etc., and then turn the information into a classroom quiz-show game. This activity is best done as a small group project.

Project Timeline

This project can take several class periods to allow time for research and game show preparation. Games can be created on the computer or created on poster board or other materials.

Variations of Idea or Add-Ons

✎ Instead of a quiz show, have students do impersonations to portray a famous actor or celebrity.

✎ Take a class period and play charades and only do movie titles.

✎ As a class, play the alphabet game and use movie titles or actor names only.

✎ Play the Famous Pairs game. This game allows students to mingle as they play detectives and learn about each other. Before the game, the teacher should write down the names of famous pairs, like Sonny and Cher, on several different cards, with each name on an individual card. Tape one name to a student's back. Students walk around asking only "yes" and "no" questions to figure out what name is written on their card and find their partner. The first two that discovers they are a pair wins the game.

✎ Instead of using pairs, you can also use famous individuals. As each student arrives, tape a three by five inch index card on their back with the name of a famous person. They must circulate in the room and ask questions that can only be answered with a "yes" or "no" to identify clues that will help them find out the name of the person on their index card. Or you can do it another way. Have the group form a circle. Give everyone a piece of masking tape and a marker. Have them write the name of a celebrity, famous person, or character on a piece of masking tape which they will stick to the forehead of the player on their left. Make sure they don't see the name. Make sure everyone can see each other's foreheads. The player's objective is to figure out who they are. Going around the circle, each payer takes a turn to ask the party questions about who they are or might be. Questions and answers must be "yes" or "no" only. If players get a "yes," they may continue asking questions to everyone. If they get a "no," the next player on the left gets to start finding out who they are. The first player to guess their name when it's their turn wins.

✎ Famous Names: Have each player choose the name of a famous person and write it down. Once the players have chosen they cannot change! Give them some examples, such as Homer Simpson, Mae West, Abraham Lincoln, Caesar Augustus, etc. Take all their names and put them in a bowl. Mix up the names and hand them out to everyone in the room. Have everyone mingle and chat while acting like their character. Better yet, have each person do thirty seconds of dialogue in the guise of the person they chose. The others guess who they are.

✎ Have students present their "Dinner Plans." Students complete the following sentence: "If I could have dinner with any person, living or dead, it would be_____ because _____."

✎ Write the word "famous" (or "movie," "actor," or "play") on the board. In groups, have students list all the movies (or celebrities) that they can think of that begin with each letter in the word.

✎ As a class, play the "Movie Name" game. The first student says a movie. The next person must say the name of a movie that starts with the last letter of the first movie. For example, the first student says, *"Jaws."* The second student must say a movie that starts with "S" ... *"Star Wars."* In this case, the third person would also say a movie that starts with "S," and so on. Instead of movies, you could also do famous celebrity names, television shows, etc.

✎ Find the Celebrity: Cut pictures of celebrity faces into four to five parts (enlarge magazine pictures or pictures from the internet on the copier). Give each student a piece of one of the pictures. On the signal, players must find their own people to make the picture complete. The first group to put their picture back together first wins.

✎ Have students complete the "Celebrity Scramble" on page 81.

Tips & Tricks

- The Microsoft site has templates you can download to create your own *Jeopardy!* game.
- Game ideas:
  - ✐ *Jeopardy!* format — create through PowerPoint, students answer in the typical, "Who is ...? What is ...?" manner.
  - ✐ *Trivial Pursuit* format — create a game board and move group tokens across spaces until they reach the end. Create categories of information.
  - ✐ Show a photo that's been blurred and has a big question mark over the top. Then read facts about the actor/actress until someone guesses who it is. Then reveal the celebrity photo.
  - ✐ Create a movie clip game show where you show short video clips from movies and the class has to name the movie.

✍ Create your game in a *"Who Wants to be a Millionaire?"* style.

✍ Use the *"Hollywood Squares"* format.

- Download PowerPoint game templates from the Internet. Just type "PowerPoint Game Templates" in your search engine.
- Play in *"Survivor"* fashion. Make flip books for the contestants and they display "True or False" or "A, B, C, D," depending on how you format your questions. Award points for correct answers. The team with the most points wins.
- Not sure where to find celebrity news? Check out a few of these sites: (Just know that some sites may not be one hundred percent reliable — but it's all in the name of fun!)

  www.celebuzz.com
  www.buzzfeed.com
  www.aceshowbiz.com
  www.facebook.com/celebritybuzz
  http://omg.yahoo.com
  www.cnn.com/SHOWBIZ/
  http://abcnews.go.com/entertainment
  www.ew.com (Entertainment Weekly)
  www.hollywoodreporter.com

  Of course your doctor's office or dentist's office may have some old *People* or *Us Weekly* magazines lying around, too!

Fun Facts

- Before she got her big break, Mariah Carey completed 500 hours of beauty school and worked as a hair sweeper in a salon, a waitress, and a coat check girl.
- Actor Russell Brand was sentenced to complete 200 hours of community service after throwing a photographer's iPhone out the window in 2012.
- According to TMZ, Mariah Carey will make close to $18 million for one year behind the judges' table on *American Idol.* Jennifer Lopez reportedly made $12 million for her first year on the show, and Britney Spears made $15 million for her duties on FOX's *The X Factor.*
- According to a list released by *Forbes Magazine,* Tom Cruise is the highest paid actor, earning $75 million between May 2011 and May 2012.

- Angelina Jolie and Sarah Jessica Parker are the highest paid actresses of 2011, earning $30 million each, according to *Forbes Magazine*. But move over Angelina and Sarah, because in 2012, Kristen Stewart topped the list at $34.5 million.
- Ashton Kutcher took over for Charlie Sheen on *Two and a Half Men* and quickly became one of the highest-paid men on television.
- Drew Carey became *The Price is Right* game show host in 2007.
- *Jeopardy!* is the winner of thirty Emmy awards, including the 2012 Emmy for Outstanding Game/Audience Participation Program.
- *Grey's Anatomy* star Patrick Dempsey began his career as a juggling, unicycle-riding clown.

Celebrity Scramble

1. uilja otsebrr _____
2. aridhrc eger _____
3. etsve nrtmia _____
4. orairsnh rfdo _____
5. cinelo naidkm _____
6. elm osibng _____
7. vhyec shaec _____
8. mdie ormeo _____
9. acjk nisholcon _____
10. tskirne ttserwa _____
11. amhwett ccmnuaehgyo _____
12. nean yaaahhtw _____
13. drab tipt _____
14. frejnnie antsion _____
15. laytor taulren _____
16. bortre sttapinno _____
17. ladien dearfflic _____
18. ashi flubaeo _____
19. neelsa zegom _____
20. finnerje realwenc _____

Celebrity Scramble Answers

1. Julia Roberts
2. Richard Gere
3. Steve Martin
4. Harrison Ford
5. Nicole Kidman
6. Mel Gibson
7. Chevy Chase
8. Demi Moore
9. Jack Nicholson
10. Kristen Stewart
11. Matthew McConaughey
12. Anne Hathaway
13. Brad Pitt
14. Jennifer Aniston
15. Taylor Lautner
16. Robert Pattinson
17. Daniel Radcliffe
18. Shia LaBeouf
19. Selena Gomez
20. Jennifer Lawrence

Chapter 16
That's Not Funny!

Chapter Objective

To give students practice in communicating with their group and making group decisions while sequencing a comic strip, otherwise known as the "funnies." They will utilize creative-thinking skills as well since they will have to determine how best to describe what they see in their piece of the strip.

Activity Overview

Students can work in groups of three or four members each. Find a comic strip from the Sunday paper and duplicate it so each group has a copy. (Don't get the paper? You can find comic strips online!) Make enough copies of the comic strip to provide one for each work group. Cut each strip into separate panels and place the panels in an envelope. Make sure you keep a copy of the uncut strips as your key for how the panels are ordered.

Steps:
1. Distribute one envelope containing a set of comic strip panels to each group.
2. Direct the members of each group to open the envelope, place the panels of the comic strip face down without examining them, and shuffle them around the table.
3. While the panels are on the table face down and hidden from view, members of each group take turns drawing a panel without showing it to others, going around until all panels have been chosen. Group members are allowed to describe their own panels as fully as possible, but they are not allowed to look at the panels of the other participants or to show their panels to others.
4. When the group members have agreed on which panel is first in the cartoon based on the participants' descriptions of the panels, they place it face down on the table. After they have placed all the panels face down in the order they have determined, they then turn them over to see if they have sequenced the comic in the proper order.

Project Timeline

This project should only take one class period.

Variations of Idea or Add-Ons

✎ Have students create a school-based cartoon strip about a hot topic at your school (such as dress code, vending machine options, cafeteria food, tardies, etc.)

✎ Have students act out their comic strip.

✎ Increase the size of the group and put multiple cut-up strips into the envelope to make it more difficult. Students will really have to be descriptive to sort it out!

✎ Play the "What Happens Next?" game. After they have assembled their strips, ask the group to brainstorm what could happen next to the characters.

✎ Have the groups ignore the dialogue on the strip and create a completely new scene by adding new dialogue.

✎ Is the comic strip a blast from the past? Have students redesign the character's outfit to be a modern-day costume.

✎ Instead of describing their panel, have the students act out or mime the panel they have selected.

Tips & Tricks

- You may be able to get newspapers from a recycling center.
- Did they finish too quickly? Have the groups switch envelopes and do it again. Repeat as necessary.
- Sponsor a "Dress as Your Favorite Funny" day in class.
- You may want to enlarge and laminate the pieces of the strip so that they can be used over and over.
- Have the students complete the "Comic Strip Trivia Challenge" on page 85.

Fun Facts

- At the height of the *Peanuts* comic strip popularity, it appeared in 2,600 newspapers and had a readership of 355 million people in seventy-five countries. It was also translated into twenty-one languages.
- *Peanuts* cartoonist Charles Schulz called his first comic strip "Li'l Folks."
- According to Encyclopedia.com, by the 1910s, the Sunday comics were so popular that newspapers would occasionally publish small books containing reprints of past strips, which they would distribute to promote the paper and gain new readers.
- The first color comic, *The Yellow Kid,* was part of the first Sunday comic section published in a 1897 newspaper. (This comic became the source of the term "yellow journalism.")
- A "gag cartoon" is a single-panel cartoon, usually including a written caption that appears beneath the drawing and most often published in magazines.

Comic Strip Trivia Challenge

1. Name Hi and Lois' kids. (Too hard? Name at least one. There are four!)
2. What title comic character serves at Camp Swampy?
3. June 19th is the birthday of what cat comic strip character?
4. What species of dog is Marmaduke?
5. What cartoon title character attends Riverdale High?
6. What cartoon character loves spinach?
7. What cartoon character always pulls the football out from Charlie Brown's foot?
8. What is the name of Blondie and Dagwood's dog?
9. Which *Peanuts* character believes in the Great Pumpkin?
10. In Peanuts, which character is always falling asleep in class?

Comic Strip Trivia Challenge Answers

1. Chip, Ditto, Dot, and Trixie
2. Beetle Bailey
3. Garfield
4. Great Dane
5. Archie
6. Popeye
7. Lucy
8. Daisy
9. Linus
10. Peppermint Patty

About the Author

This is Rebecca Young's eighth drama book for teens and her first book of drama projects. This was a fun journey away from her normal monologues, duologues, and play manuscripts.

For many years, Rebecca wrote and directed drama for middle school and high school students for her church. She cofounded a Christian acting group called "One Voice." It was a dream of hers to combine writing, acting, and helping youth.

Rebecca currently works in a totally "non-dramatic" profession as a Systems Analyst at Central Bank in Lexington, Kentucky. She has a Bachelor of Arts degree in Communications/Marketing from the University of Kentucky. (But she's not one of the crazy UK basketball fans that you see on TV — don't tell anyone!)

She lives in Kentucky with her three daughters, Heather, Kristina, and Ashley, and her son-in-law, Chris. To round out the family, she has two cats who basically rule the house.

Whether you are an actor or a writer, she suggests this anonymous quote as a daily mantra: "You aren't finished when you lose; you are finished when you quit."

Never give up hope.